LONDON:
T. F. A. DAY, 13, CAREY STREET, AND 3, NEW COURT,
LINCOLN'S INN, W.C.

PREFACE.

The history of Chess Problems—a delightful subject, by the way—has yet to be written, and we are uninformed of the extent to which this beautiful off-shoot of the parent game was cultivated in former times. At no period, however, in all probability has the attention of so many Chess Amateurs been devoted either to the production or to the solution of these ingenious puzzles, as in the present day. Chess Problems are now, indeed, a distinct branch of Chess study. This is undoubtedly due in a great measure to the immense impulse given to Chess a few years since, but it is partly owing, also, to the more attractive character of the compositions themselves. The earlier collections of Chess Problems consist largely of positions of the nature of what are called "End-games," positions in which, so long as the resemblance to a real game was preserved, little pains were taken to limit the number of moves required to effect the mate. Many of them, again, are of the "suicidal" kind, and others are clogged by special and perplexing stipulations. By degrees the ingenuities of Chess Problem composers have become limited to a narrower range, " self-mates," mates in 250 moves; mates with a particular Pawn, or on a particular square; mates in " not more and not less" than a specified number of moves, have given way to the easier, but far more useful positions of three, four, or five moves only. Of the Chess Problem in this its latest and most captivating form, many strikingly beautiful examples have appeared of late years in periodicals that devote a column of their space to Chess, and judging from the favourable reception they have met, this henceforth will doubtless be the class of positions permanently and generally in vogue.

Among those who have ministered most ably and bountifully to the popular craving for this description of Chess stratagem, Mr. John Brown, or, as he preferred to write himself " J. B., of Bridport," the author of this collection has long stood pre-eminent.

The productions of this regretted gentleman, who died recently in the prime of manhood, are remarkable for a degree of unvarying excellence, which has never been, perhaps, surpassed. Some of his rivals have composed finer problems than any in these pages, but their genius manifestly ebbed and flowed, while his seems always to have been at height. There is not a single diagram of this composer deficient in point and beauty. He has no feeble or indifferent plots, and he never fritters away his idea in elaborating it into a problem. All is ornate and finished, to a high degree, and are most unlike those ruins of good conceptions sometimes discoverable in meagre pieces of strategy.

The constancy, too, with which he keeps to his high standing, is the more admirable, and the more praiseworthy, from the fact of his uniform accuracy. Composers and examiners of Chess Problems know, all too well, that errors *will* elude their utmost vigilance, but "J. B." subjected his inventions to such rigid scrutiny that scarcely one ever left his hand imperfect.

Another merit in these problems, of a different kind, is their variety. The Author, had, it is true, his favourite combinations, and sometimes fondly returned to the same theme for the purpose of embodying it skilfully in a new composition; but his conceptions are generally as fresh as they are vigorous. As a rule he does not crowd his diagrams, and he rarely gives the defending side a studied superiority of force. In nearly every case the solution is made to hinge on an ingenious *coup de repos*, branching thence into numerous variations, each of which is itself a skilful enigma. His predilection for combinations of the Queen and Knights, or of Queen, Knight, and Bishop, is well exemplified in Nos. 32, 65, 39, and 47. Among the three-move positions, which form more than two thirds of this collection, there will be found many charming stratagems. Where all are so good, however, it is difficult to make selections. Still, without saying absolutely they are the best, particular attention may be invited to Nos. 51, 66, 71, 92, 98, 113, 122, 125, 130. No. 9, is one of the most exquisite two-move problems known, and those who are at the pains to study Nos. 144, 163, and that master-piece, No. 173, will regret that there are not more positions of four, and five moves depth in the book.

A volume of Chess Problems so meritorious as these of Mr. Brown carries its own recommendation, and can hardly fail of a welcome wherever the game which it serves so beautifully to illustrate is known. This posthumous collection, has, however, another claim to consideration, and one which will be irresistible to Chess players of generous sympathies. It is published solely for the benefit of the widow and orphans of its estimable Author.

ERRATUM.

In Problem No. 18, Two White Kings have been inserted. The King
on the Knight's pawn square should be a WHITE QUEEN.

₊ In explanation of the fact that three or four of the diagrams in this
volume are repetitions of preceding diagrams, it is proper to mention that
many of Mr. Brown's Problems were printed in several periodicals, and
have been collected by different hands.

PROBLEM No. 1.

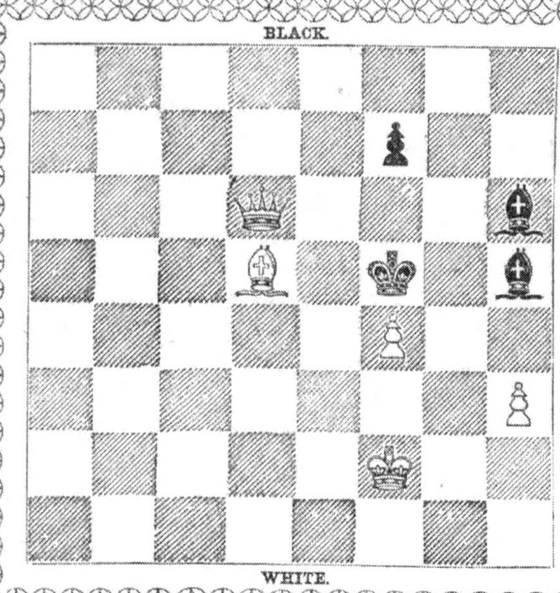

White to play and mate in two moves.

PROBLEM No. 2.

White to play and mate in two moves.

PROBLEM No. 3.

White to play and mate in two moves.

PROBLEM No. 4.

White to play and mate in two moves.

PROBLEM No. 5.

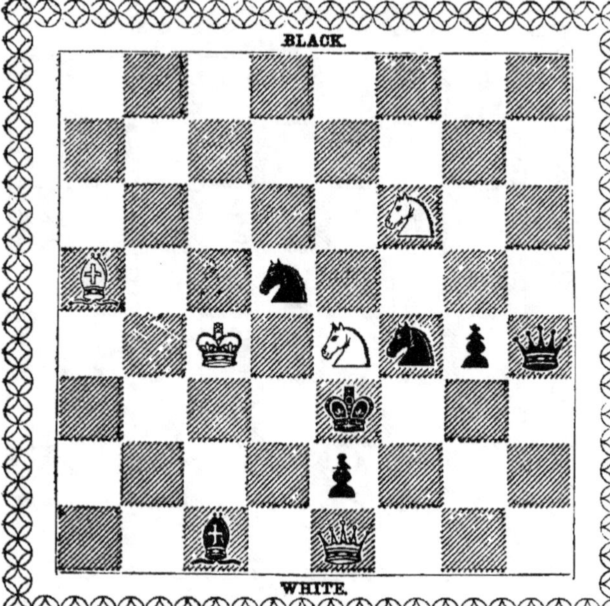

White to play and mate in two moves.

PROBLEM No. 6.

White to play and mate in two moves.

PROBLEM No. 7.

White to play and mate in two moves.

PROBLEM No. 8.

White to play and mate in two moves.

PROBLEM No. 9.

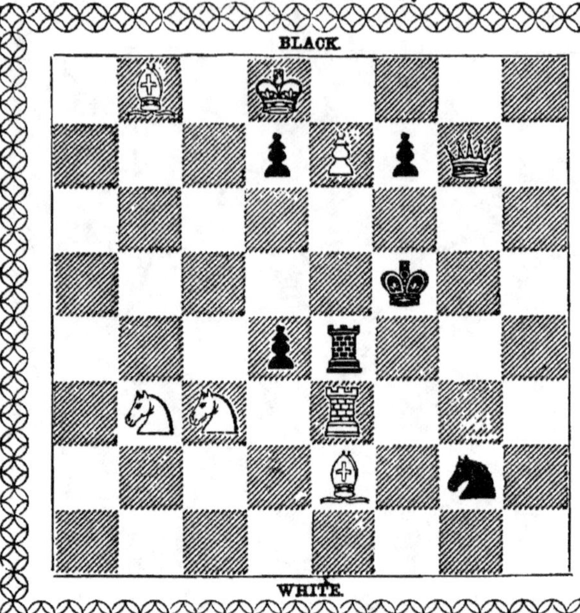

White to play and mate in two moves.

PROBLEM No. 10.

White to play and mate in three moves.

PROBLEM No. 11.

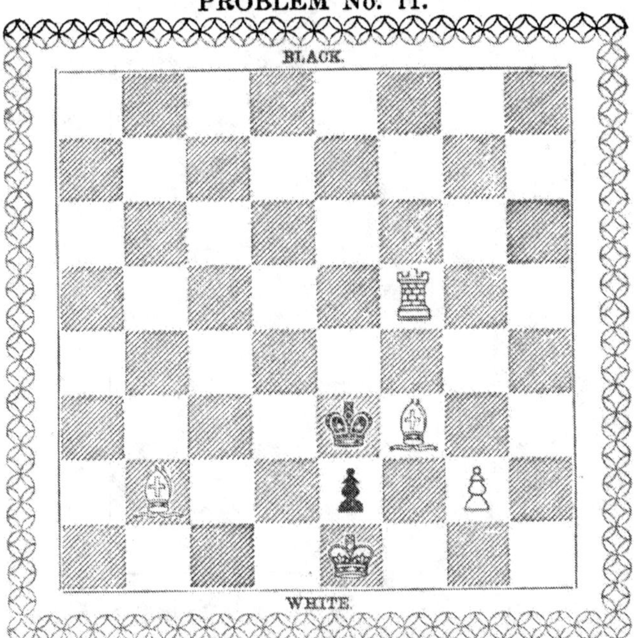

White to play and mate in three moves.

PROBLEM No. 12.

White to play and mate in three moves.

PROBLEM No. 13.

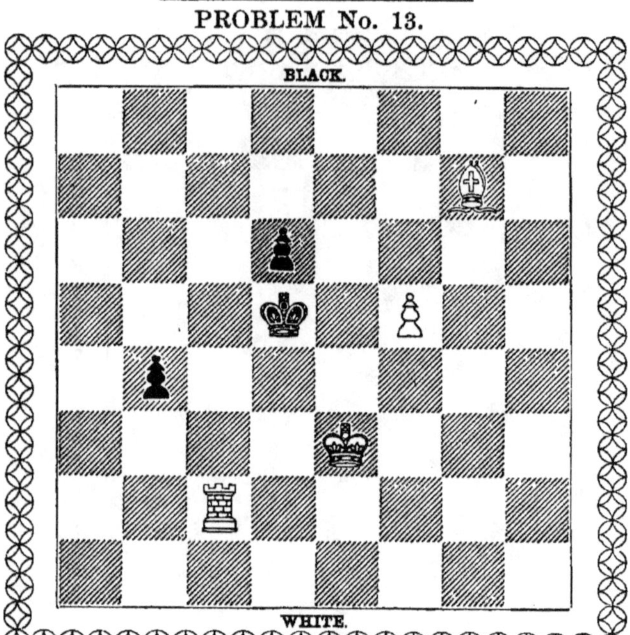

White to play and mate in three moves.

PROBLEM No. 14.

White to play and mate in three moves.

PROBLEM No. 15.

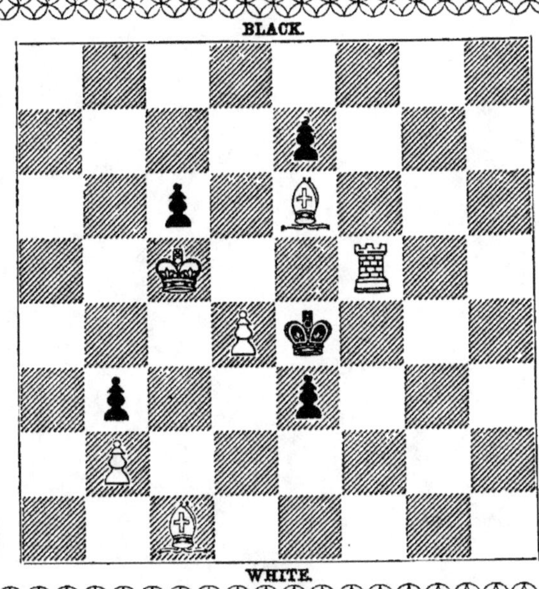

White to play and mate in three moves.

PROBLEM No. 16.

White to play and mate in three moves.

PROBLEM No. 17.

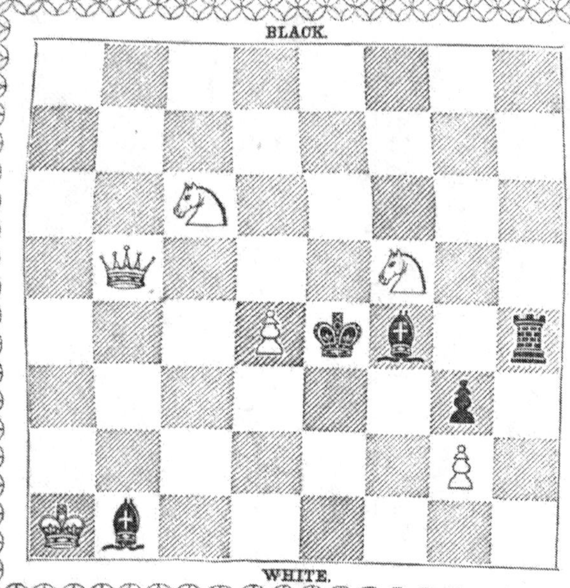

White to play and mate in three moves.

PROBLEM No. 18.

White to play and mate in three moves.

PROBLEM No. 19.

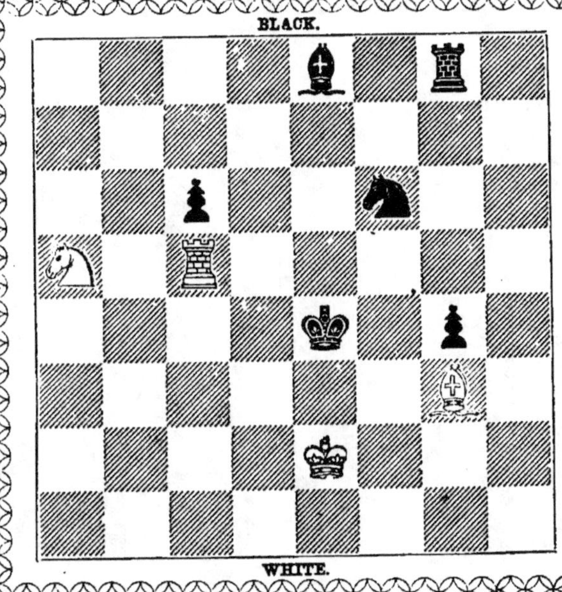

White to play and mate in three moves.

PROBLEM No. 20.

White to play and mate in three moves.

PROBLEM No. 21.

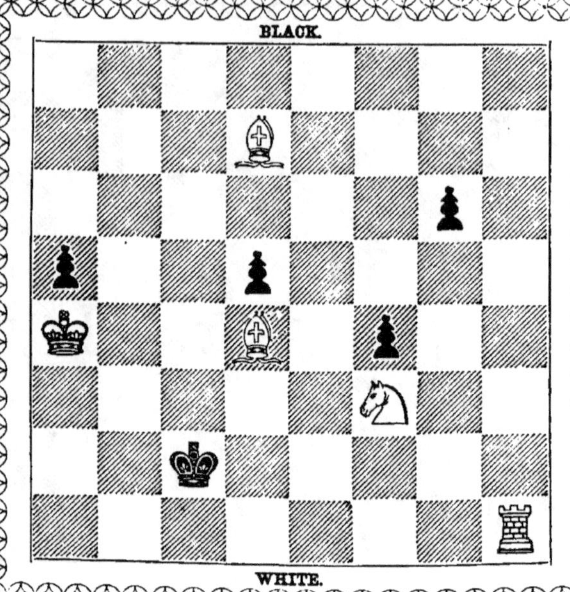

White to play and mate in three moves.

PROBLEM No. 22.

White to play and mate in three moves.

PROBLEM No. 23.

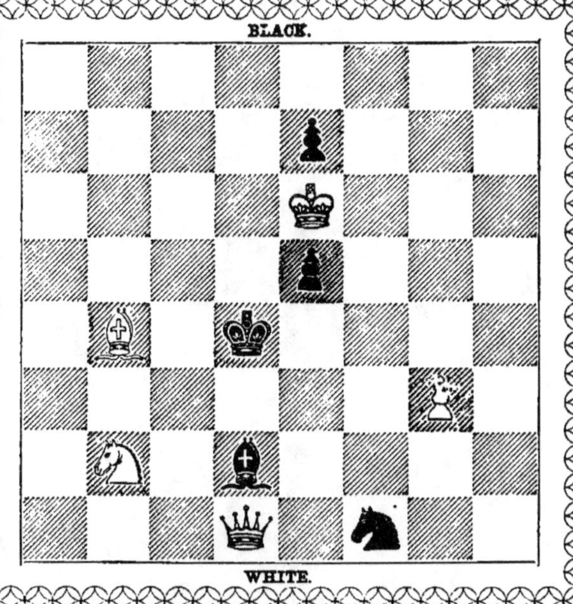

White to play and mate in three moves.

PROBLEM No. 24.

White to play and mate in three moves.

PROBLEM No. 25.

White to play and mate in three moves.

PROBLEM No. 26.

White to play and mate in three moves.

PROBLEM No. 27.

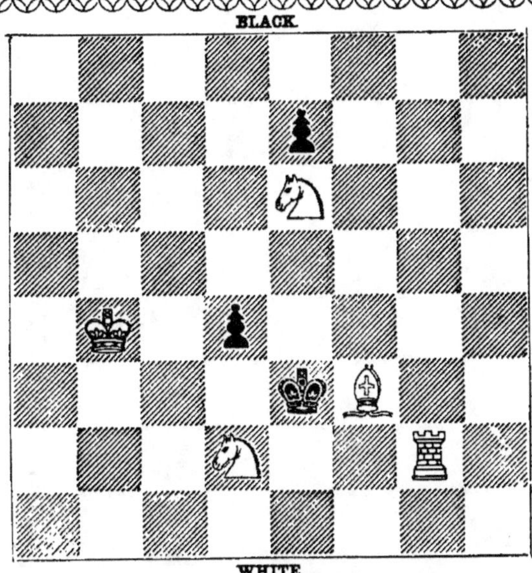

White to play and mate in three moves.

PROBLEM No. 28.

White to play and mate in three moves.

PROBLEM No. 29.

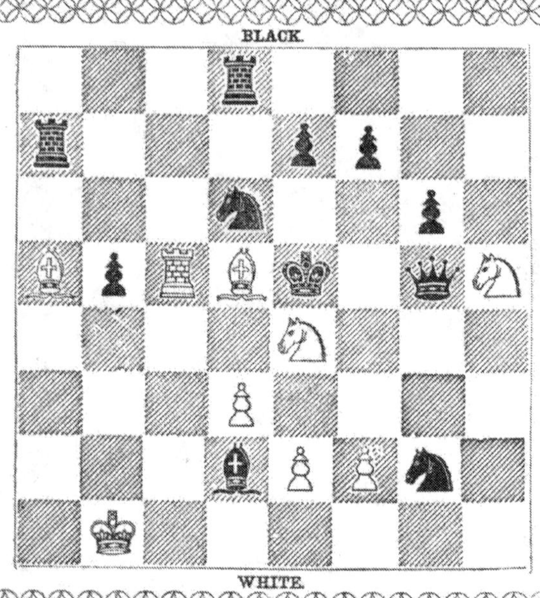

White to play and mate in three moves.

PROBLEM No. 30.

White to play and mate in three moves.

PROBLEM No. 31.

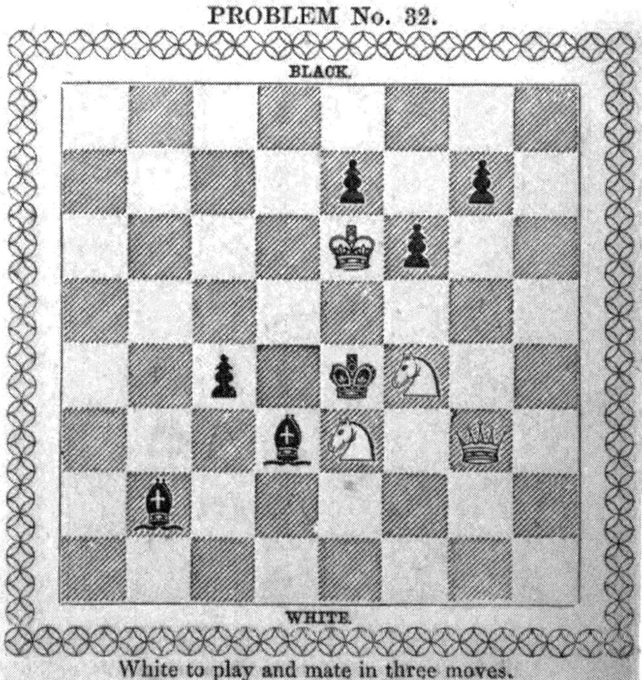

White to play and mate in three moves.

PROBLEM No. 32.

White to play and mate in three moves.

PROBLEM No. 33.

White to play and mate in three moves.

PROBLEM No. 34.

White to play and mate in three moves.

PROBLEM No. 35.

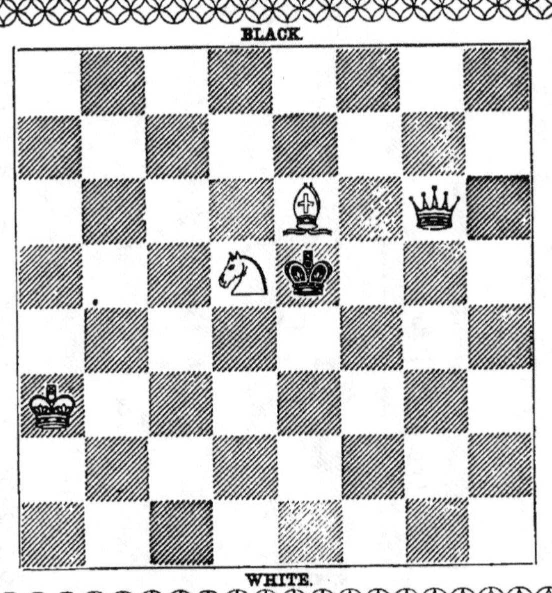

White to play and mate in three moves.

PROBLEM No. 36.

White to play and mate in three moves.

PROBLEM No. 37.

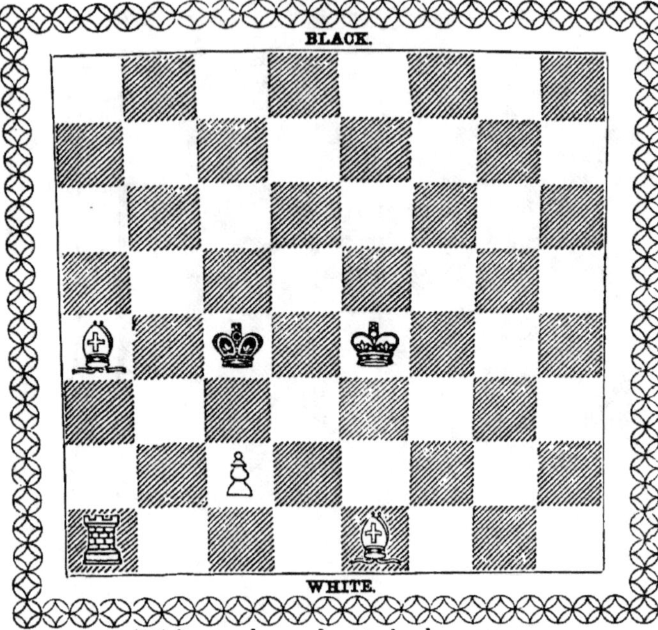

White to play and mate in three moves.

PROBLEM No. 38.

White to play and mate in three moves.

PROBLEM No. 39.

White to play and mate in three moves.

PROBLEM No. 40.

White to play and mate in three moves.

PROBLEM No. 41.

White to play and mate in three moves.

PROBLEM No. 42.

White to play and mate in three moves.

PROBLEM No. 43.

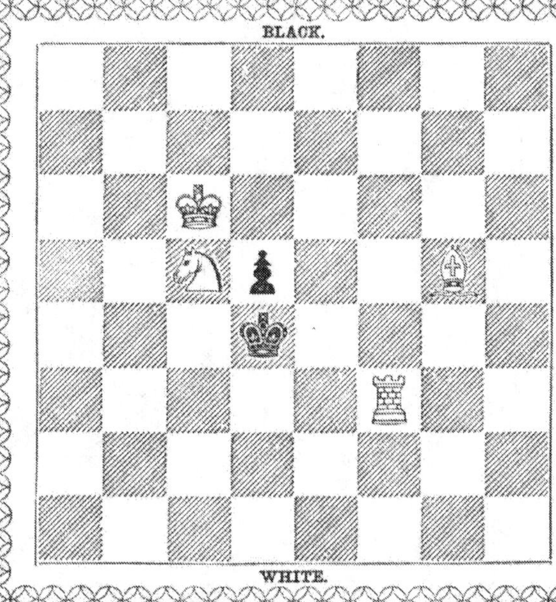

White to play and mate in three moves.

PROBLEM No. 44.

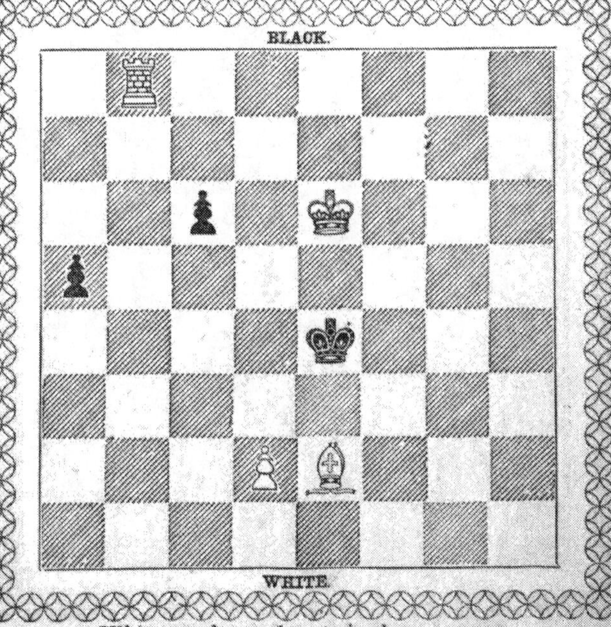

White to play and mate in three moves.

PROBLEM No. 45.

White to play and mate in three moves.

PROBLEM No. 46.

White to play and mate in three moves.

PROBLEM No. 47.

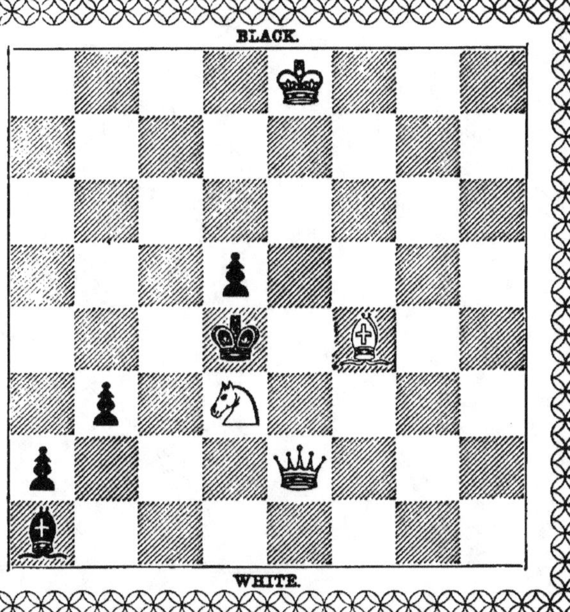

White to play and mate in three moves.

PROBLEM No. 48.

White to play and mate in three moves.

PROBLEM No. 49.

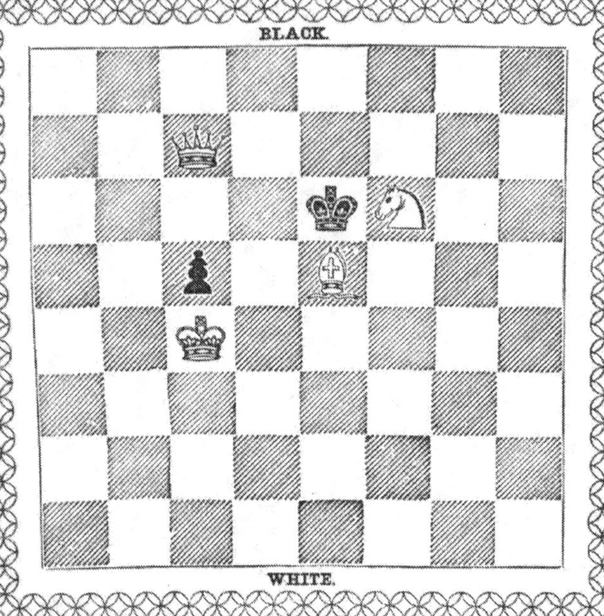

White to play and mate in three moves.

PROBLEM No. 50.

White to play and mate in three moves.

PROBLEM No. 51.

White to play and mate in three moves.

PROBLEM No. 52.

White to play and mate in three moves.

PROBLEM No. 53.

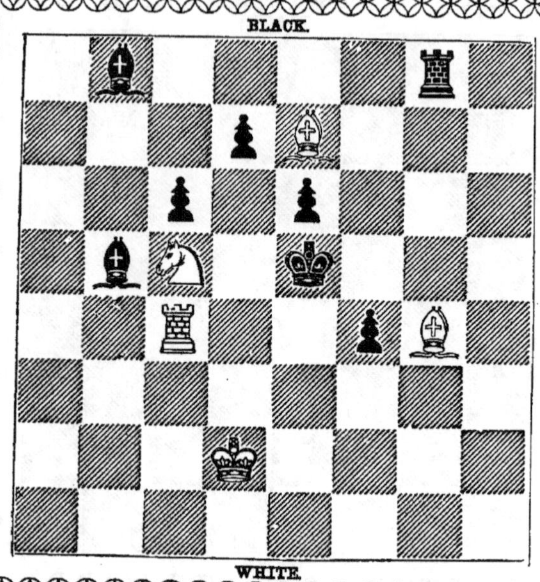

White to play and mate in three moves.

PROBLEM No. 54.

White to play and mate in three moves.

PROBLEM No. 55.

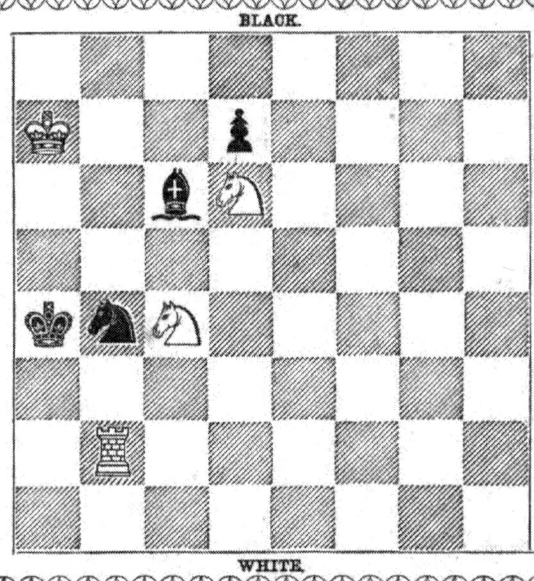

White to play and mate in three moves.

PROBLEM No. 56.

White to play and mate in three moves.

PROBLEM No. 57.

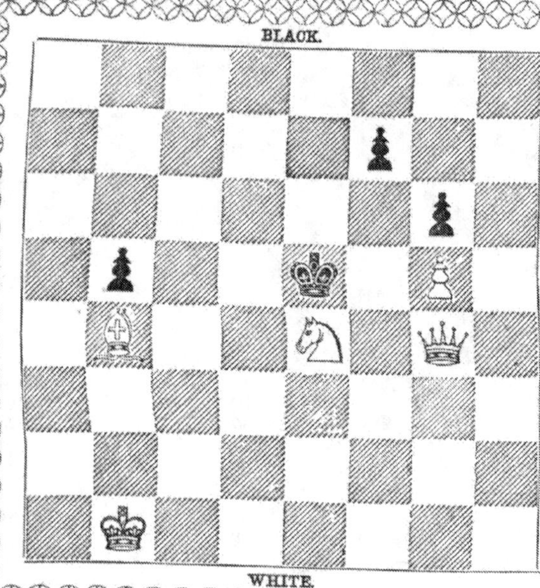

White to play and mate in three moves.

PROBLEM No. 58.

White to play and mate in three moves.

PROBLEM No. 59.

White to play and mate in three moves.

PROBLEM No. 60.

White to play and mate in three moves.

PROBLEM No. 61.

White to play and mate in three moves.

PROBLEM No. 62.

White to play and mate in three moves.

PROBLEM No. 63.

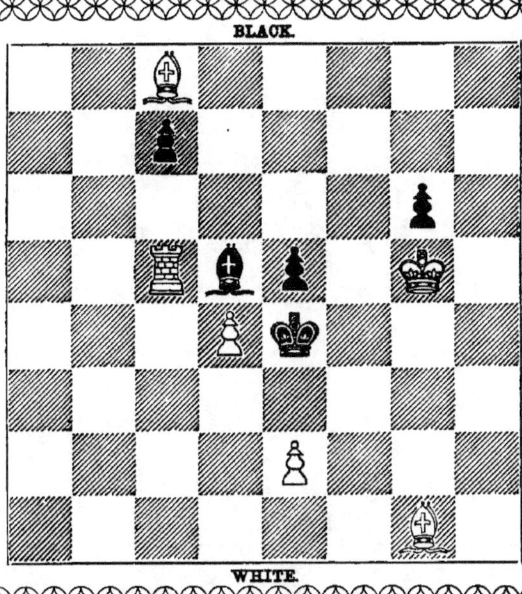

White to play and mate in three moves.

PROBLEM No. 64.

White to play and mate in three moves.

PROBLEM No. 65.

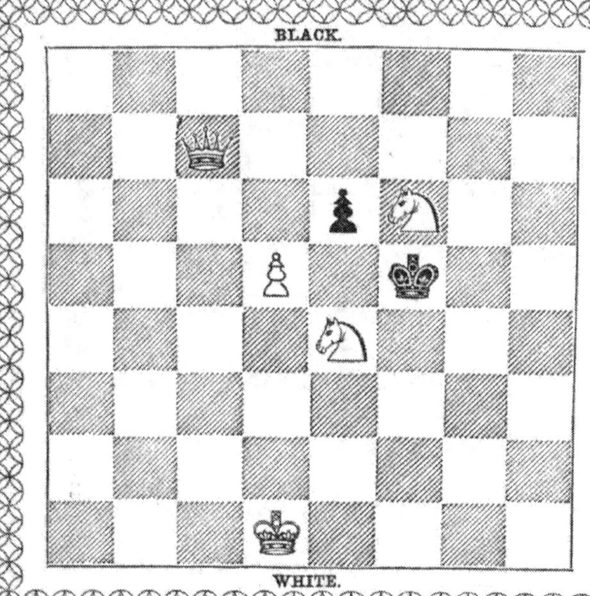

White to play and mate in three moves.

PROBLEM No. 66.

White to play and mate in three moves.

PROBLEM No. 67.

White to play and mate in three moves.

PROBLEM No. 68.

White to play and mate in three moves.

PROBLEM No. 69.

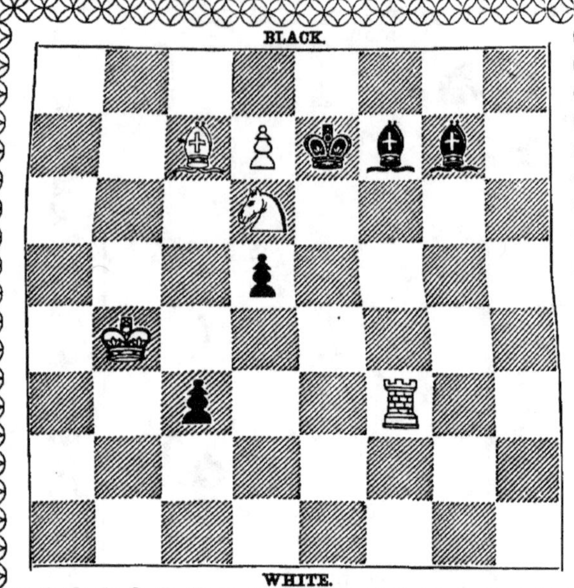

White to play and mate in three moves.

PROBLEM No. 70.

White to play and mate in three moves.

PROBLEM No. 71.

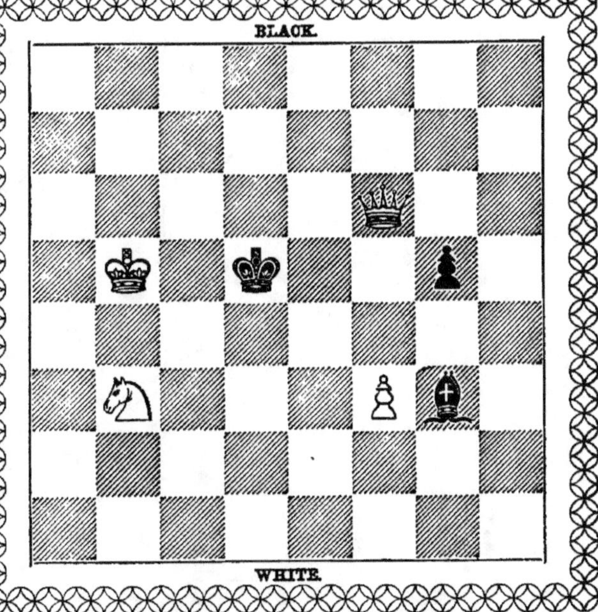

White to play and mate in three moves.

PROBLEM No. 72.

White to play and mate in three moves.

PROBLEM No. 73.

White to play and mate in three moves.

PROBLEM No. 74.

White to play and mate in three moves.

PROBLEM No. 75.

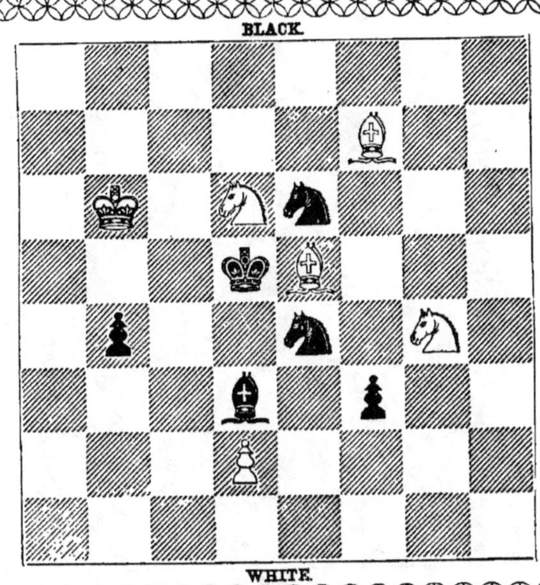

White to play and mate in three moves.

PROBLEM No. 76.

White to play and mate in three moves.

PROBLEM No. 77.

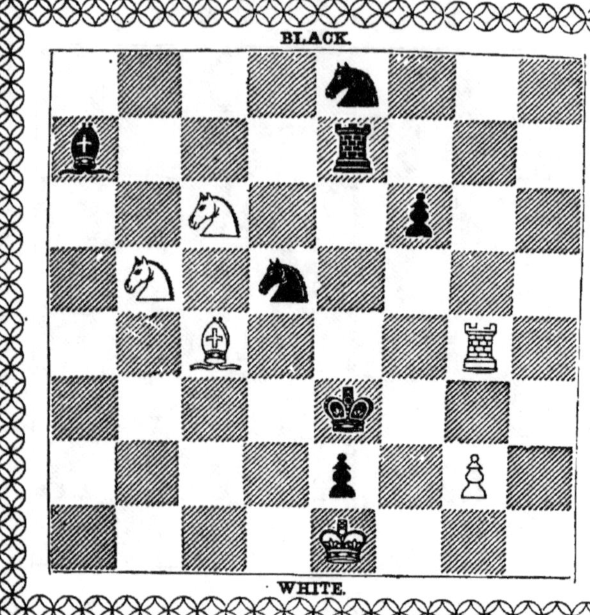

White to play and mate in three moves.

PROBLEM No. 78.

White to play and mate in three moves.

PROBLEM No. 79.

White to play and mate in three moves.

PROBLEM No. 80.

White to play and mate in three moves.

PROBLEM No. 81.

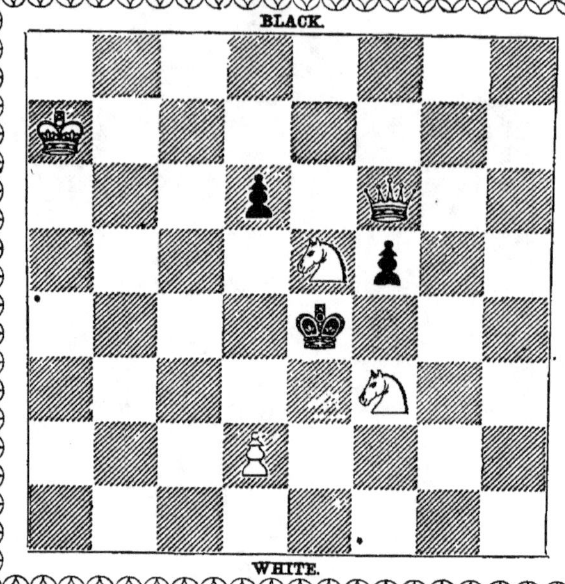

White to play and mate in three moves.

PROBLEM No. 82.

White to play and mate in three moves.

PROBLEM No. 83.

White to play and mate in three moves.

PROBLEM No. 84.

White to play and mate in three moves.

PROBLEM No. 85.

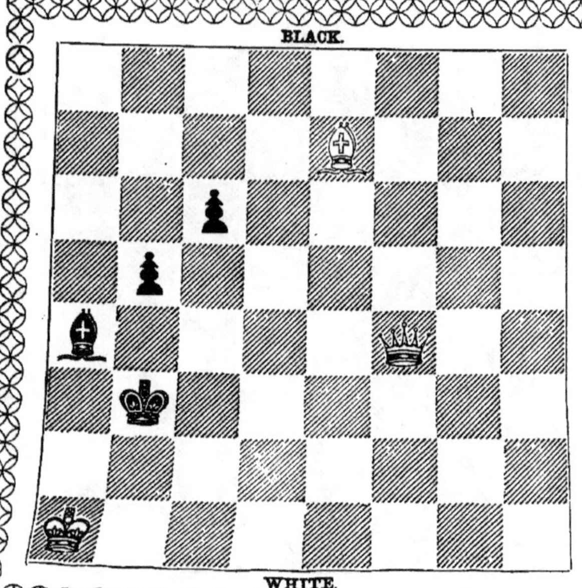

White to play and mate in three moves.

PROBLEM No. 86.

White to play and mate in three moves.

PROBLEM No. 87.

White to play and mate in three moves.

PROBLEM No. 88.

White to play and mate in three moves.

PROBLEM No. 89.

White to play and mate in three moves.

PROBLEM No. 90.

White to play and mate in three moves.

PROBLEM No. 91.

White to play and mate in three moves.

PROBLEM No. 92.

White to play and mate in three moves.

PROBLEM No. 93.

White to play and mate in three moves.

PROBLEM No. 94.

White to play and mate in three moves.

PROBLEM No. 95.

White to play and mate in three moves.

PROBLEM No. 96.

White to play and mate in three moves.

PROBLEM No. 97.

White to play and mate in three moves.

PROBLEM No. 98.

White to play and mate in three moves.

PROBLEM No. 99.

White to play and mate in three moves.

PROBLEM No. 100.

White to play and mate in three moves.

PROBLEM No. 101.

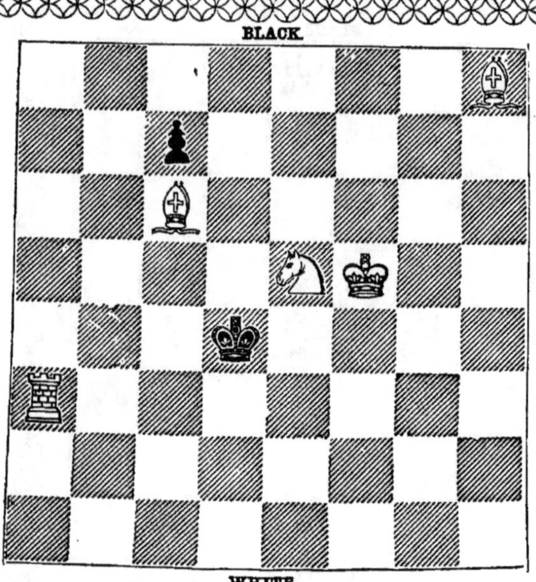

White to play and mate in three moves.

PROBLEM No. 102.

White to play and mate in three moves.

PROBLEM No. 103.

White to play and mate in three moves.

PROBLEM No. 104.

White to play and mate in three moves.

PROBLEM No. 105.

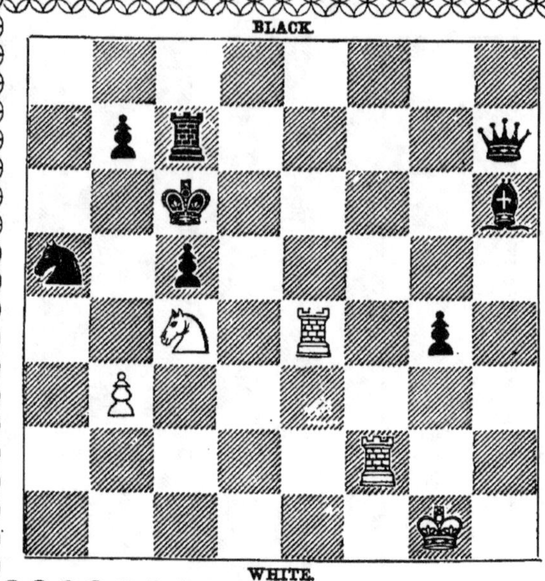

White to play and mate in three moves.

PROBLEM No. 106.

White to play and mate in three moves.

PROBLEM No. 107.

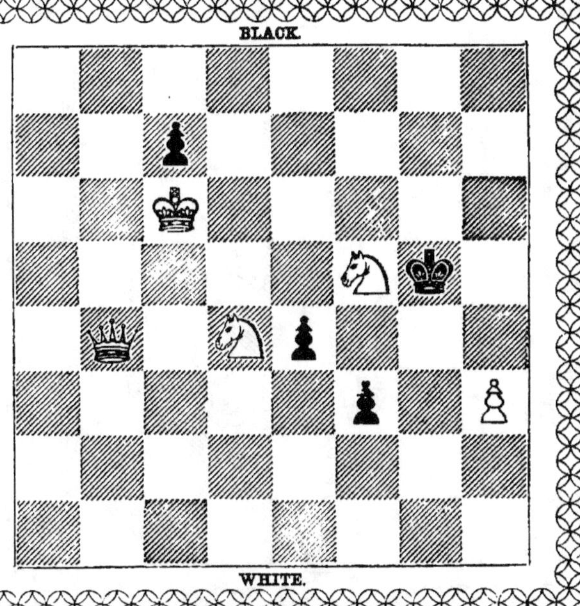

White to play and mate in three moves.

PROBLEM No. 108.

White to play and mate in three moves.

PROBLEM No. 109.

White to play and mate in three moves.

PROBLEM No. 110.

White to play and mate in three moves.

PROBLEM No. 111.

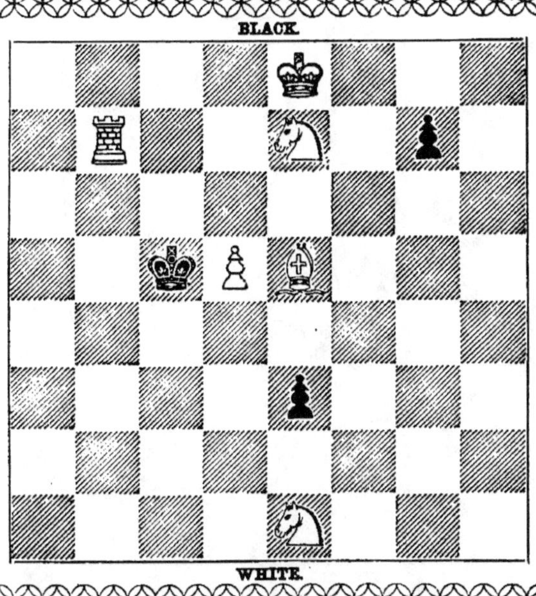

White to play and mate in three moves.

PROBLEM No. 112.

White to play and mate in three moves.

PROBLEM No. 113.

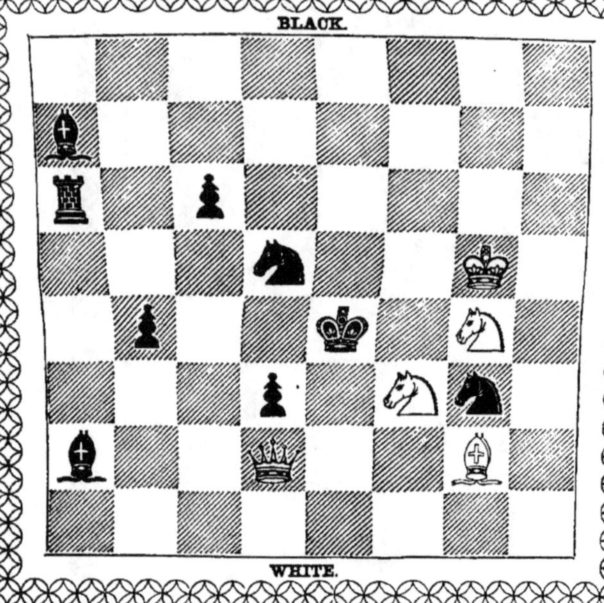

White to play and mate in three moves.

PROBLEM No. 114.

White to play and mate in three moves.

PROBLEM No. 115.

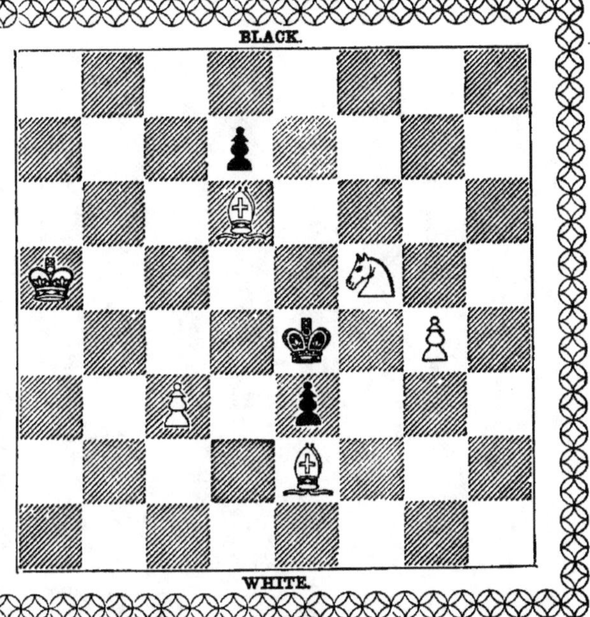

White to play and mate in three moves.

PROBLEM No. 116.

White to play and mate in three moves.

PROBLEM No. 117.

White to play and mate in three moves.

PROBLEM No. 118.

White to play and mate in three moves.

PROBLEM No. 119.

White to play and mate in three moves.

PROBLEM No. 120.

White to play and mate in three moves.

PROBLEM No. 121.

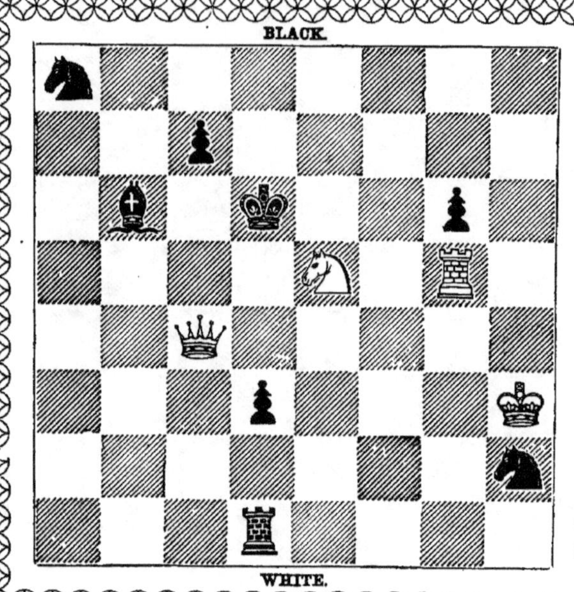

White to play and mate in three moves.

PROBLEM No. 122.

White to play and mate in three moves.

PROBLEM No. 123.

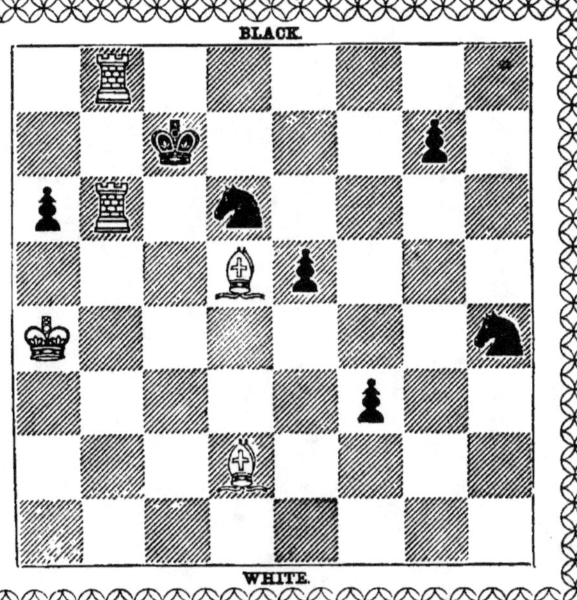

White to play and mate in three moves.

PROBLEM No. 124.

White to play and mate in three moves.

PROBLEM No. 125.

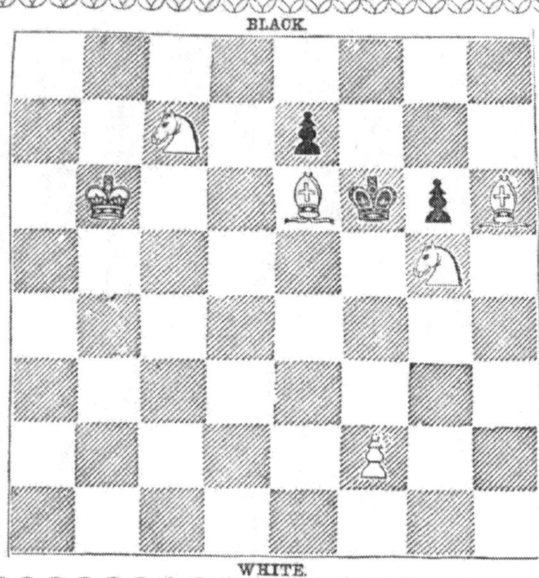

White to play and mate in three moves.

PROBLEM No. 126.

White to play and mate in three moves.

PROBLEM No. 127.

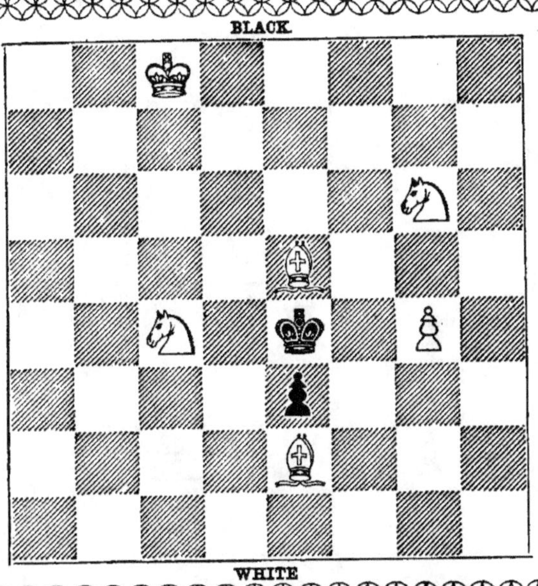

White to play and mate in three moves.

PROBLEM No. 128.

White to play and mate in three moves.

PROBLEM No. 129.

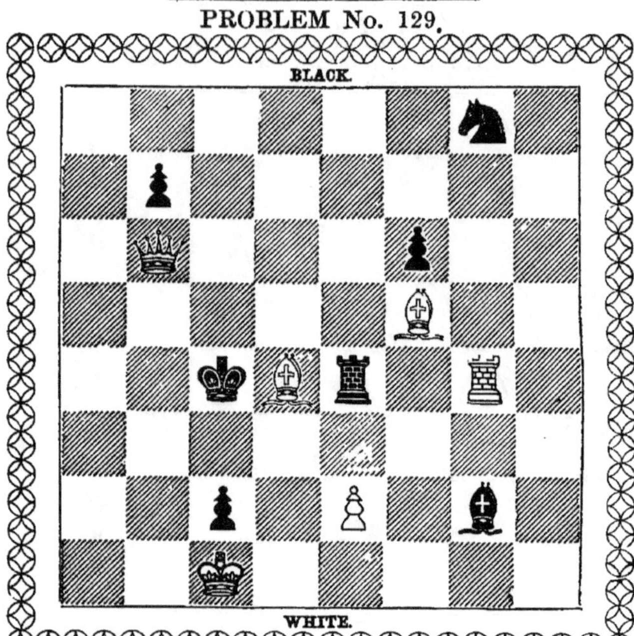

White to play and mate in three moves.

PROBLEM No. 130.

White to play and mate in three moves.

PROBLEM No. 131.

White to play and mate in three moves.

PROBLEM No. 132.

White to play and mate in three moves.

PROBLEM No. 133.

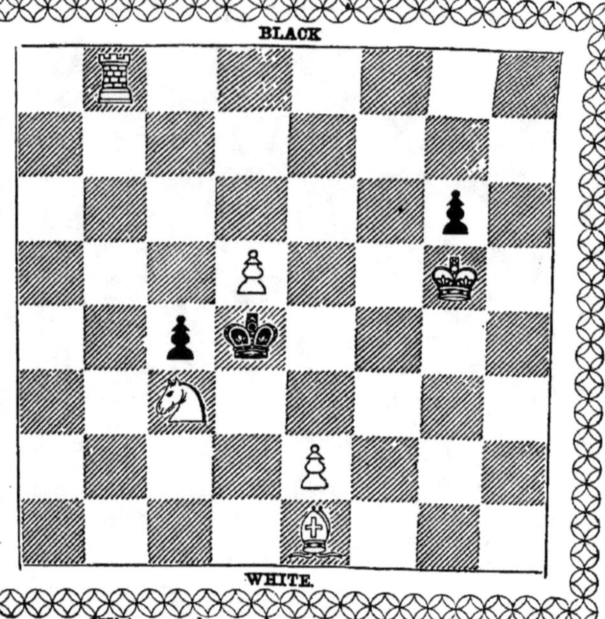

White to play and mate in four moves.

PROBLEM No. 134.

White to play and mate in four moves.

PROBLEM No. 135.

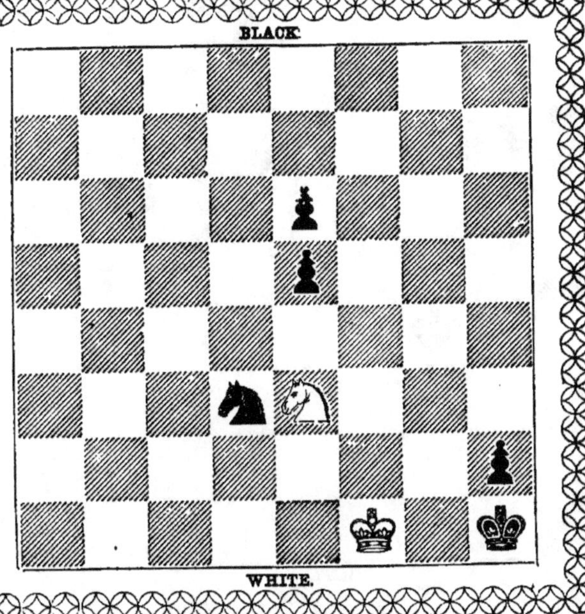

White to play and mate in four moves.

PROBLEM No. 136.

White to play and mate in four moves.

PROBLEM No. 137.

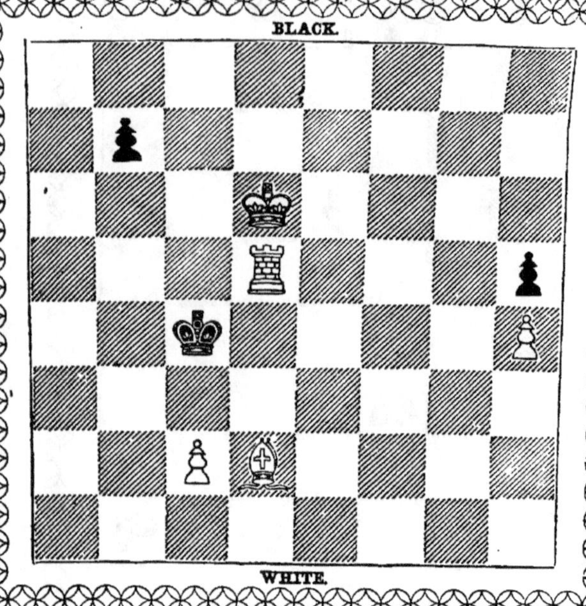

White to play and mate in four moves.

PROBLEM No. 138.

White to play and mate in four moves.

PROBLEM No. 139.

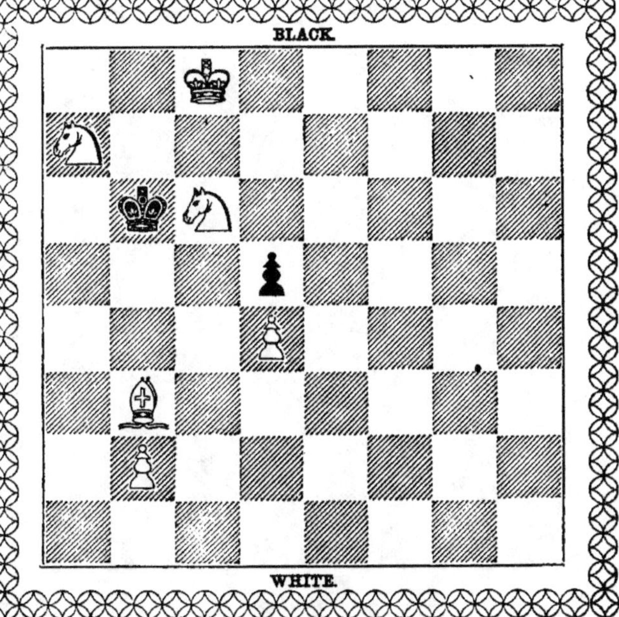

White to play and mate in four moves.

PROBLEM No. 140.

White to play and mate in four moves.

PROBLEM No. 141.

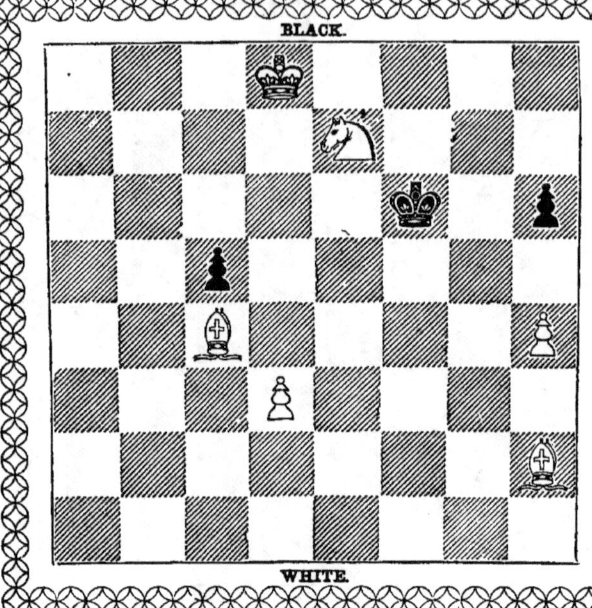

White to play and mate in four moves.

PROBLEM No. 142.

White to play and mate in four moves.

PROBLEM No. 143.

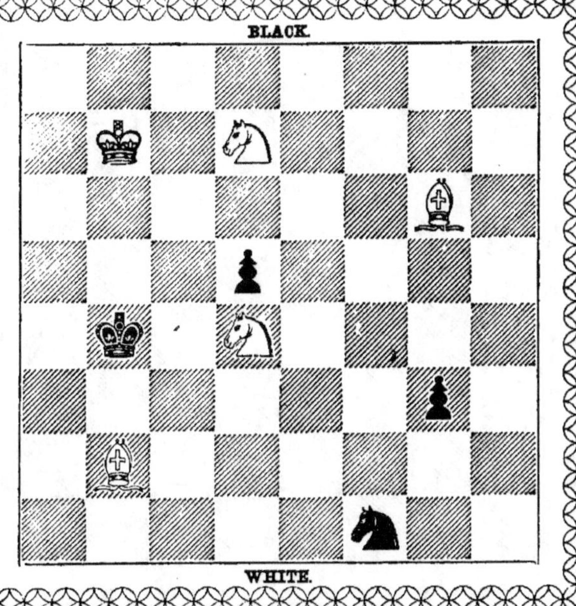

White to play and mate in four moves.

PROBLEM No. 144.

White to play and mate in four moves.

PROBLEM No. 145.

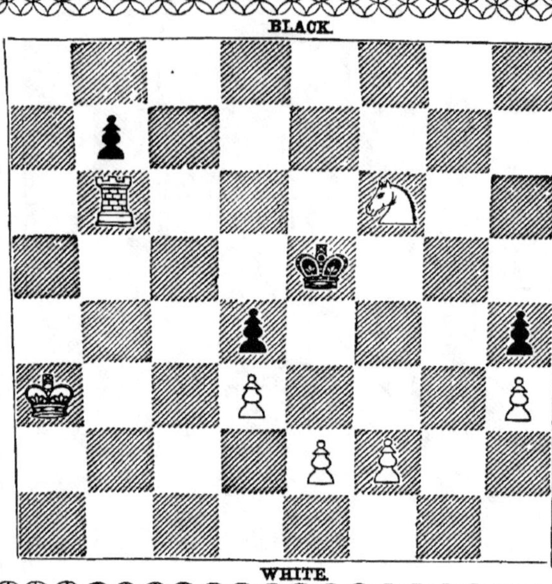

White to play and mate in four moves.

PROBLEM No. 146.

White to play and mate in four moves.

PROBLEM No. 147.

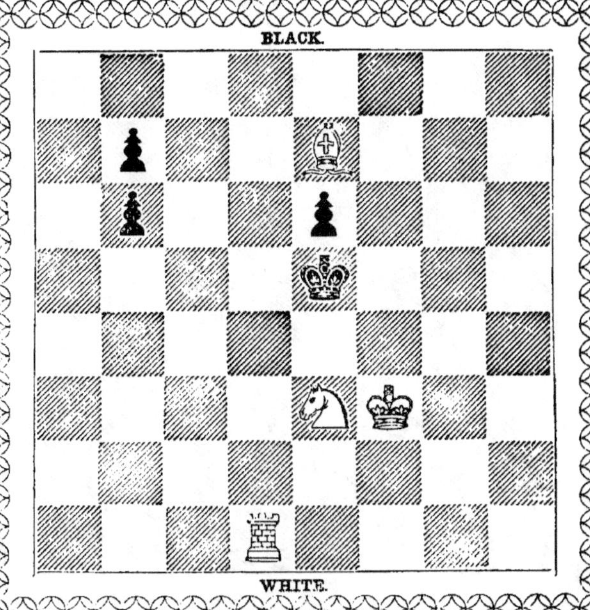

White to play and mate in four moves.

PROBLEM No. 148.

White to play and mate in four moves.

PROBLEM No. 149.

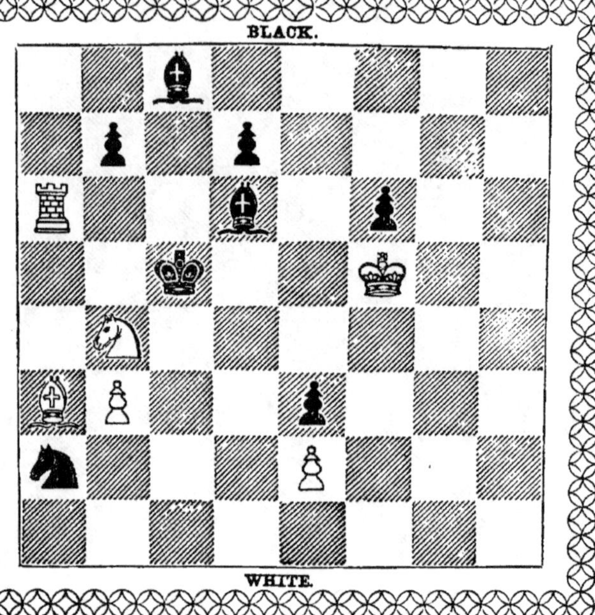

White to play and mate in four moves.

PROBLEM No. 150.

White to play and mate in four moves.

PROBLEM No. 151.

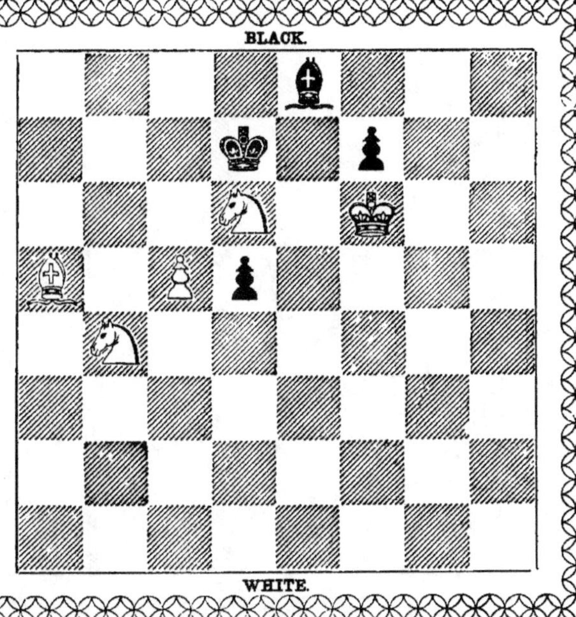

White to play and mate in four moves.

PROBLEM No. 152.

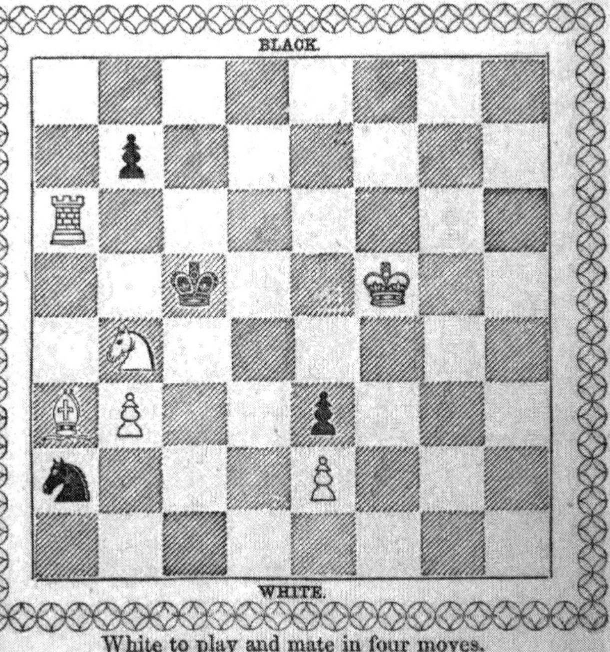

White to play and mate in four moves.

PROBLEM No. 153.

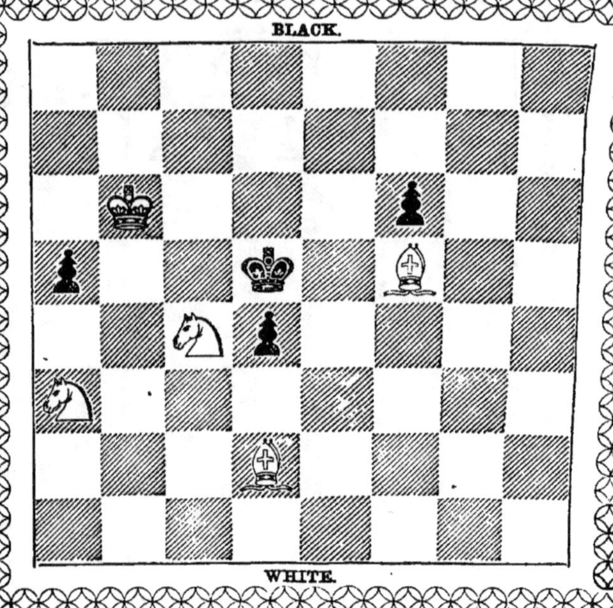

White to play and mate in four moves.

PROBLEM No. 154.

White to play and mate in four moves.

PROBLEM No. 155.

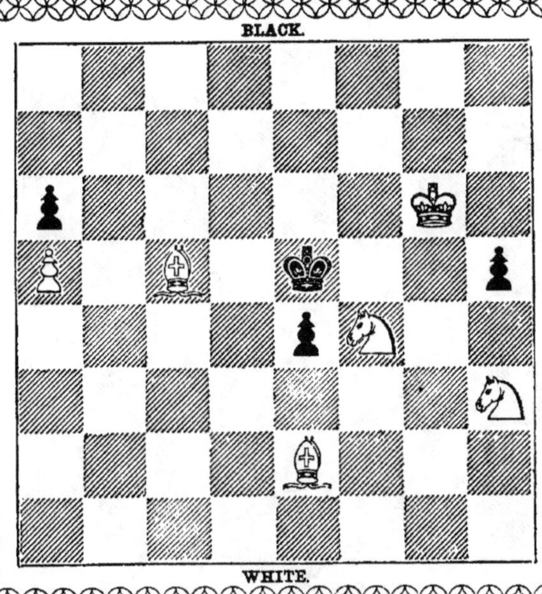

White to play and mate in four moves.

PROBLEM No. 156.

White to play and mate in four moves.

PROBLEM No. 157.

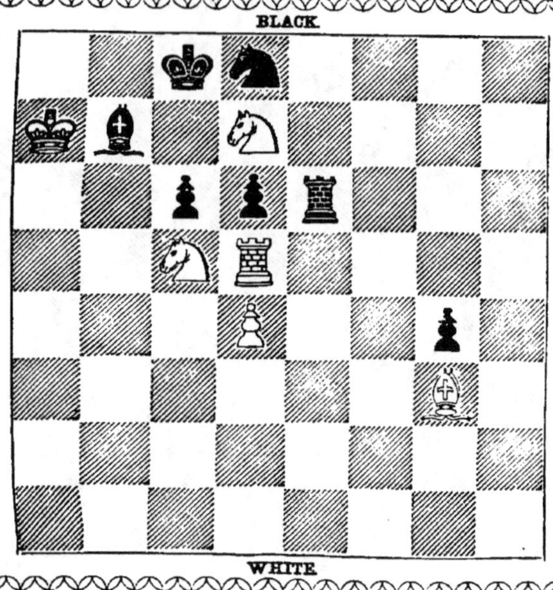

White to play and mate in four moves.

PROBLEM No. 158.

White to play and mate in four moves.

PROBLEM No. 159.

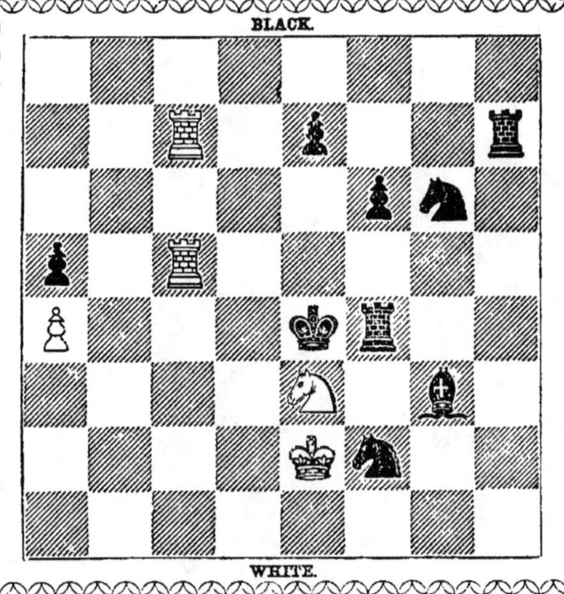

White to play and mate in four moves.

PROBLEM No. 160.

White to play and mate in four moves.

PROBLEM No. 161.

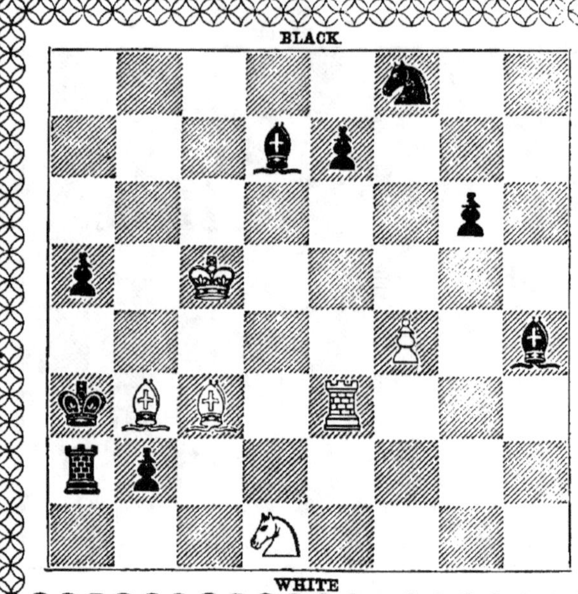

White to play and mate in four moves.

PROBLEM No. 162.

White to play and mate in four moves.

PROBLEM No. 163.

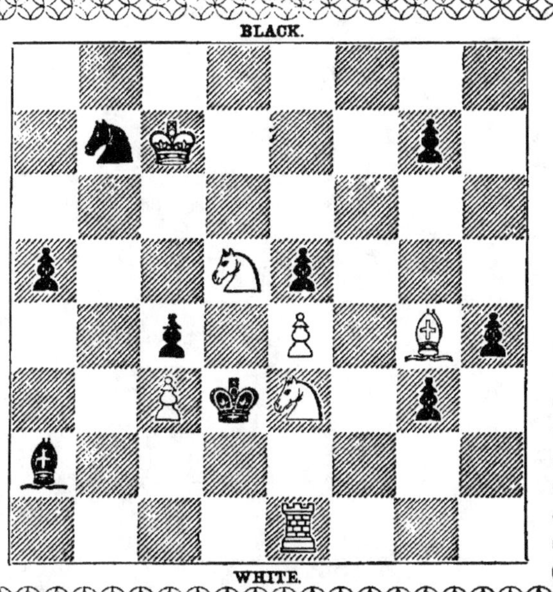

White to play and mate in four moves.

PROBLEM No. 164.

White to play and mate in four moves.

PROBLEM No. 165.

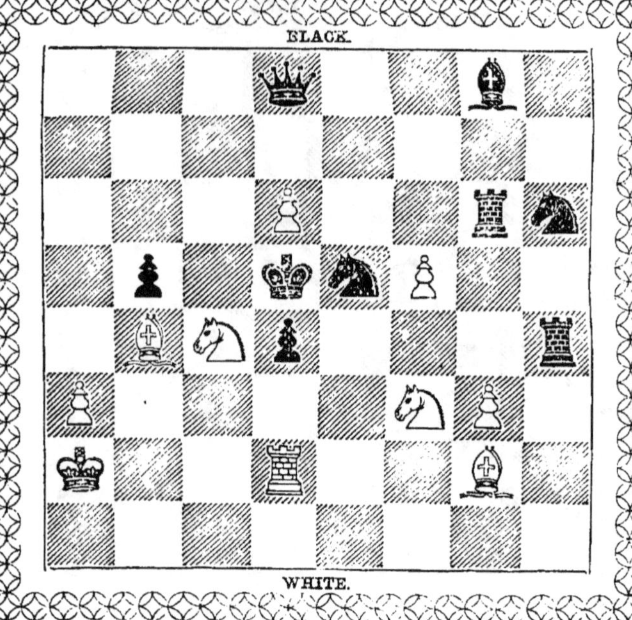

White to play and mate in four moves.

PROBLEM No. 166.

White to play and mate in four moves.

PROBLEM No. 167.

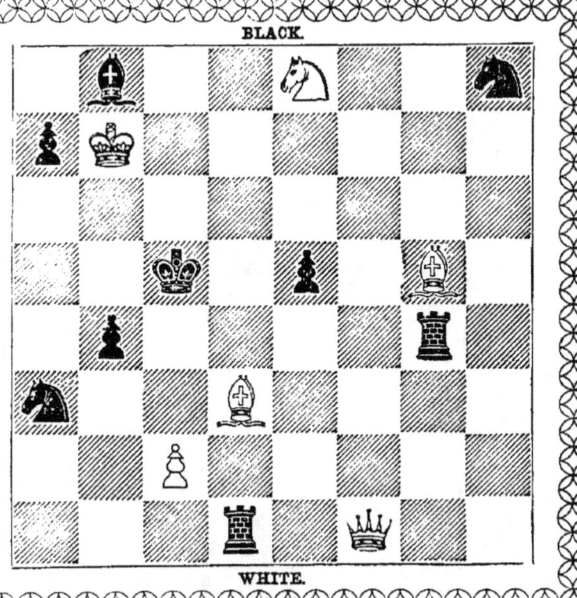

White to play and mate in four moves.

PROBLEM No. 168.

White to play and mate in five moves.

PROBLEM No. 169.

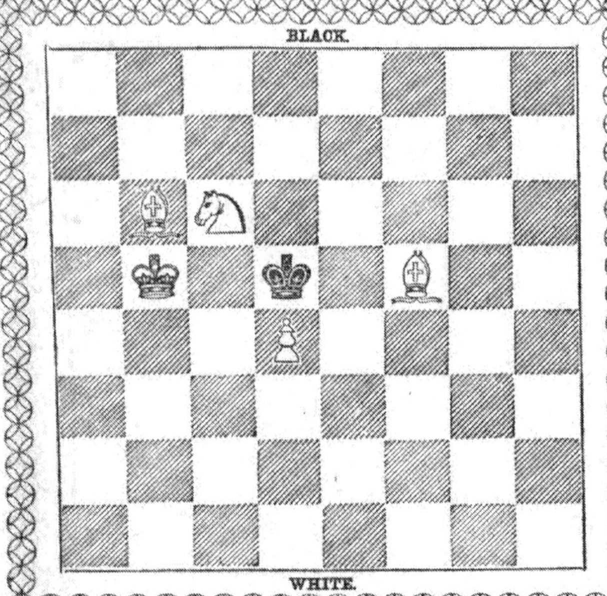

White to play and mate in five moves.

PROBLEM No. 170.

White to play and mate in five moves.

PROBLEM No. 171.

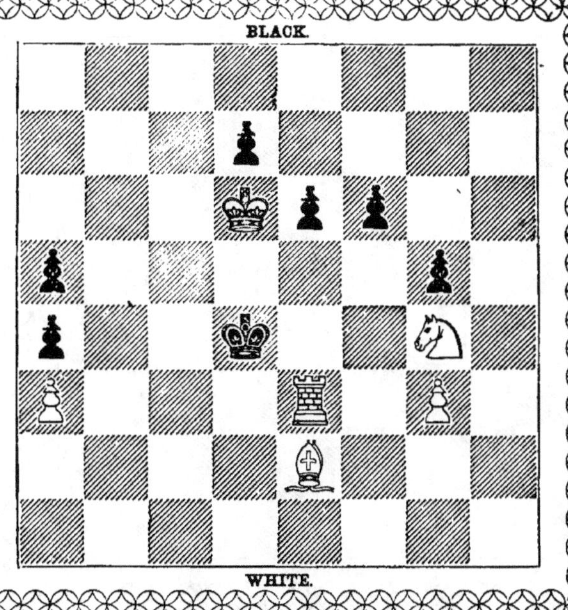

White to play and mate in five moves.

PROBLEM No. 172.

White to play and mate in five moves.

PROBLEM No. 173.

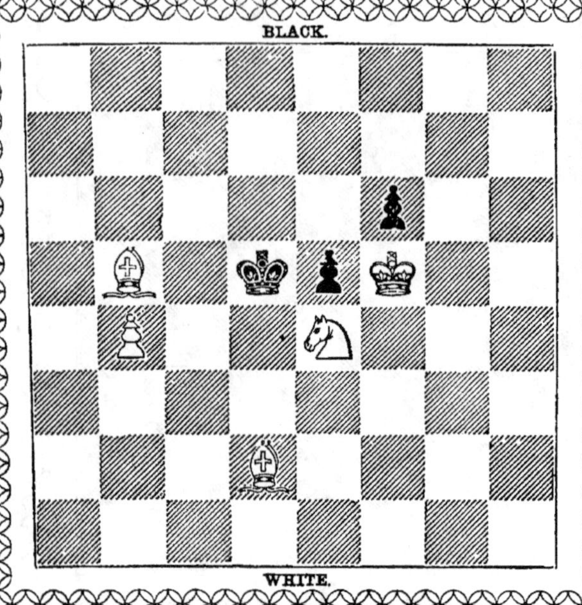

White to play and mate in five moves.

PROBLEM No. 174.

White to play and mate in five moves.

SOLUTIONS.

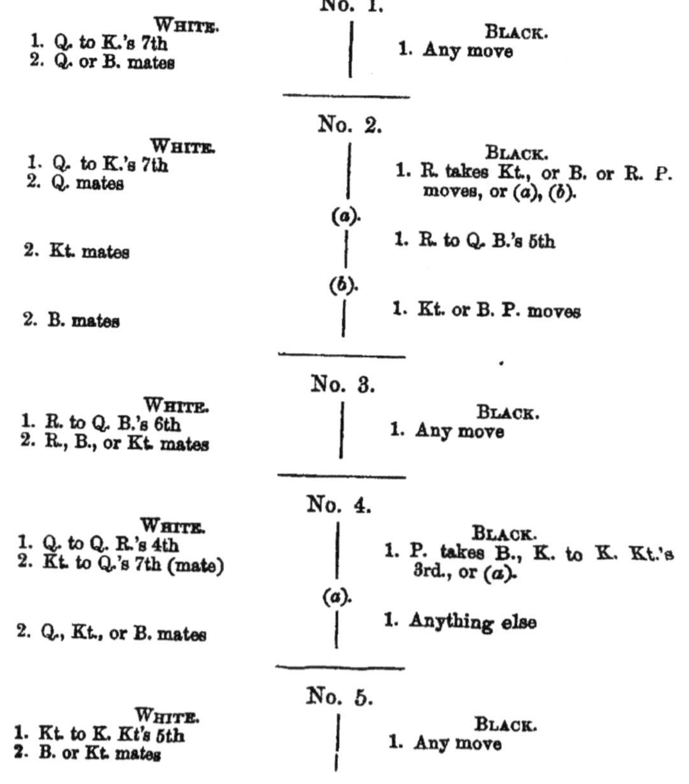

No. 1.

WHITE.	BLACK.
1. Q. to K.'s 7th	1. Any move
2. Q. or B. mates	

No. 2.

WHITE.	BLACK.
1. Q. to K.'s 7th	1. R. takes Kt., or B. or R. P. moves, or (a), (b).
2. Q. mates	

(a).

	1. R. to Q. B.'s 5th
2. Kt. mates	

(b).

	1. Kt. or B. P. moves
2. B. mates	

No. 3.

WHITE.	BLACK.
1. R. to Q. B.'s 6th	1. Any move
2. R., B., or Kt. mates	

No. 4.

WHITE.	BLACK.
1. Q. to Q. R.'s 4th	1. P. takes B., K. to K. Kt.'s 3rd., or (a).
2. Kt. to Q.'s 7th (mate)	

(a).

	1. Anything else
2. Q., Kt., or B. mates	

No. 5.

WHITE.	BLACK.
1. Kt. to K. Kt's 5th	1. Any move
2. B. or Kt. mates	

No. 6.

WHITE.	BLACK.
1. R. to Q.'s 6th	1. Any move
2. R., B., Kt., or P. mates	

No. 7.

WHITE.	BLACK.
1. Q. to K. Kt's sq.	1. Any move
2. Q. or B. mates	

No. 8.

WHITE.	BLACK.
1. Kt. to K.'s 6th	1. Any move
2. R., B., or Kt. mates	

No. 9.

WHITE.	BLACK.
1. B. to K. B.'s 4th	1. K. takes B. or (a), (b), (c)
2. R. to K. B.'s 3rd, mating	

(a).

	BLACK.
	1. K. to K.'s 3rd
2. Kt. takes P. (mate)	

(b).

	BLACK.
	1. R. takes B.
2. R. to K.'s 5th (mate)	

(c).

	BLACK.
	1. R. moves otherwise
2. Q. mates	

There are many other beautiful variations, but with a like result.

No. 10.

WHITE.	BLACK.
1. Kt. to K. B.'s. 4th	1. K. moves
2. R. to K. R.'s 5th	2. K. takes Kt.
3. R. mates	

No. 11.

WHITE.	BLACK.
1. P. to Kt.'s 3rd	1. K. moves
2. R. to Q. Kt.'s 5th	2. K. moves
3. R. or B. mates	

No. 12.

WHITE.	BLACK.
1. R. to Q. B.'s 2nd (ch.)	1. K. to Q.'s 6th (best)
2. Q. to K. R.'s 2nd	2. Any move
3. Q. mates	

No. 13.

WHITE.	BLACK.
1. B. to Q. Kt.'s 2nd	1. P. moves
2. R. to Q. B.'s 3rd	2. K. moves
3. R. to B.'s 5th, (double check, and mate)	

No. 14.

WHITE.	BLACK.
1. R. to Q. B.'s 5th	1. K. to Q.'s 5th, or P. to K.'s 3rd, or (a)
2. R. to Q. B.'s 6th	2. Any move
3. R. mates	

(a).

	1. K. to K.'s 6th
2. R. to Q. B.'s 2nd, (dis. ch.)	2. K. moves
3. R. to K.'s 2nd, mating	

No. 15.

WHITE.	BLACK.
1. R. to K. B.'s 7th or 8th	1. K. to Q.'s 6th
2. R. to K. B.'s sq.	2. Any move
3. B. mates	

No. 16.

WHITE.	BLACK.
1. Q. to Q.'s 8th	1. Kt. to Q. Kt.'s 3rd, (best)
2. B. to K.'s 5th	2. Any move
3. Q. or B. mates	

No. 17.

WHITE.	BLACK.
1. Kt. to Q. K.'s 4th	1. B. to Q.'s 3rd
2. Q. to K. B.'s sq.	2. Any move
3, Q. mates	

No. 18.

WHITE.	BLACK.
1. Q. to K. R.'s 3rd	1. B. takes Kt., (best)
2. Q. to K.'s 6th	2. Any move
3. Q. or B. mates	

No. 19.

WHITE.	BLACK.
1. Kt. to Q. Kt.'s 7th	1. K. moves, or (a)
2. B. to K.'s 5th	2. K. moves
3. Kt. mates	

(a).

	1. R. to K. Kt.'s 4th, or Kt. to Q.'s 4th
2. Kt. checks	2. K. moves
3. B. or R. mates	

No. 20.

WHITE.	BLACK.
1. B. to Q. Kt.'s 3rd	1. B. to Q.'s 4th
2. Kt. to K.'s 4th	2. Any move
3. B., Kt., or P. mates	

No. 21.

WHITE.	BLACK.
1. B. to K. Kt.'s 4th	1. K. moves
2. R. checks	2. K. to Q. B.'s 7th, or 5th, or K.'s 5th or 7th
3. Kt. mates	

No. 22.

WHITE.	BLACK.
1. Q. to Q.'s 6th	1. B. to K. Kt.'s 4th, or (a), (b)
2. B. to K. Kt.'s 7th	2. Any move
3. Q. mates	

(a).

	1. B. to Q. Kt.'s 2nd
2. B. to K. R.'s 6th	2. Any move.
3. Q. mates	

(b).

	1. B. to K.'s 3rd
2. Q. takes P. (ch.)	2. K. to K. B.'s 5th
3. B. to Q.'s 6th, (mate)	

No. 23.

WHITE.	BLACK.
1. Q. to K.'s 2nd	1. P. moves (best)
2. Q. to Q.'s square	2. Anywhere
3. Q, or B. mates	

No. 24.

WHITE.	BLACK.
1. Q. to K.'s B.'s 3rd	1. P. to K.'s 5th (best)
2. Q. to Q.'s sq.	2. Any move
3. Q. mates	

No. 25.

WHITE.	BLACK.
1. Kt. to Q.'s 4th	1. P. to B.'s 5th, or (a)
2. B. to K. Kt.'s 4th	2. Any move
3. Kt. mates	

(a).

	1. Any other move
2. Kt. takes P.	2. Any move
3. R. or B. mates	

No. 26.

WHITE.	BLACK.
1. B. to K.'s 2nd	1. P. takes B.
2. R. checks	2. Any move
3. R. or P. mates	

No. 27.

WHITE.	BLACK.
1. Kt. takes P.	1. Any move
2. Kt. to Q.'s B.'s 4th	2. Any move
3. R. mates	

No. 28.

WHITE.	BLACK.
1. R. to Q.'s 4th	1. Kt. takes R. (best)
2. Kt. to K.'s 3rd	2. Either Kt. moves
3. Kt. mates	

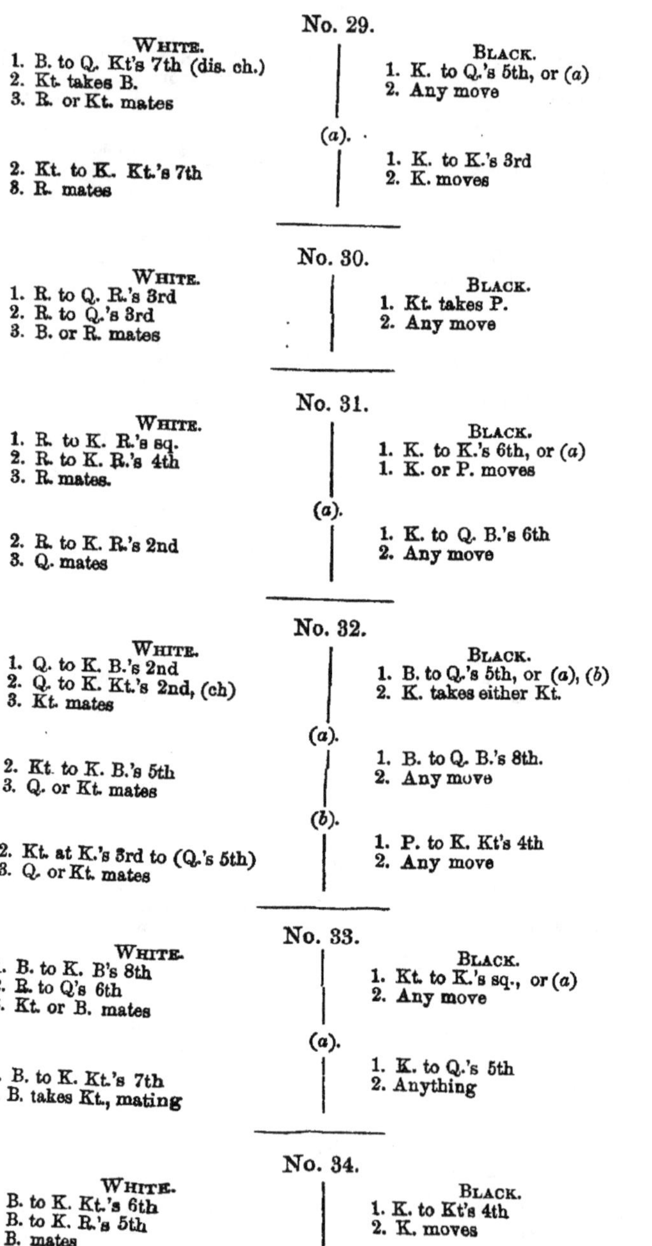

No. 29.

WHITE.
1. B. to Q. Kt's 7th (dis. ch.)
2. Kt. takes B.
3. R. or Kt. mates

BLACK.
1. K. to Q.'s 5th, or (a)
2. Any move

(a).

2. Kt. to K. Kt.'s 7th
8. R. mates

1. K. to K.'s 3rd
2. K. moves

No. 30.

WHITE.
1. R. to Q. R.'s 3rd
2. R. to Q.'s 3rd
3. B. or R. mates

BLACK.
1. Kt. takes P.
2. Any move

No. 31.

WHITE.
1. R. to K. R.'s sq.
2. R. to K. R.'s 4th
3. R. mates.

BLACK.
1. K. to K.'s 6th, or (a)
1. K. or P. moves

(a).

2. R. to K. R.'s 2nd
3. Q. mates

1. K. to Q. B.'s 6th
2. Any move

No. 32.

WHITE.
1. Q. to K. B.'s 2nd
2. Q. to K. Kt.'s 2nd, (ch)
3. Kt. mates

BLACK.
1. B. to Q.'s 5th, or (a), (b)
2. K. takes either Kt.

(a).

2. Kt. to K. B.'s 5th
3. Q. or Kt. mates

1. B. to Q. B.'s 8th.
2. Any move

(b).

2. Kt. at K.'s 3rd to (Q.'s 5th)
3. Q. or Kt. mates

1. P. to K. Kt's 4th
2. Any move

No. 33.

WHITE.
1. B. to K. B's 8th
2. R. to Q's 6th
3. Kt. or B. mates

BLACK.
1. Kt. to K.'s sq., or (a)
2. Any move

(a).

2. B. to K. Kt.'s 7th
3. B. takes Kt., mating

1. K. to Q.'s 5th
2. Anything

No. 34.

WHITE.
1. B. to K. Kt.'s 6th
2. B. to K. R.'s 5th
3. B. mates

BLACK.
1. K. to Kt's 4th
2. K. moves

(94)

No. 35.

WHITE.	BLACK.
1. Q. to K. R.'s 6th	1. K. moves
2. Q. to K.'s 3rd	2. K. moves
3. Q. or Kt. mates	

No. 36.

WHITE.	BLACK.
1. Kt. to Q. R.'s 4th	1. K. moves
2. P. to K.'s 4th	2. K. moves
3. B. mates	

No. 37.

WHITE.	BLACK.
1. B. to Q.'s 7th	1. K. moves
2. R. to Q. R.'s 7th	2. K. moves
3. R. or B. mates	

No. 38.

WHITE.	BLACK.
1. B. to K. R.'s 7th	1. Any move
2. R. takes K. B. P.	2. Any move
3. R. to K. B.'s 3rd, or to K.'s 5th, 6th, or 7th (mate)	

No. 39.

WHITE.	BLACK.
1. Q. to Q. R.'s 7th	1. Any move
2. Kt. to K.'s 6th	2. Any move
3. Q. or B. mates	

No. 40.

WHITE.	BLACK.
1. Kt. from Kt's 4th to Q.'s 3rd	1. P. moves, or (a)
2. Q. to K. R.'s 6th	2. K. moves
3. Q. mates	

(a).

WHITE.	BLACK.
	1. K. to Kt's 4th
2. Q. to Q. R.'s 2nd	2. Anything
3. Q. mates	

No. 41.

WHITE.	BLACK.
1. Q. to K. R.'s sq.	1. K. to K.'s 4th, or (a)
2. Q. to K. R.'s 4th	2. K. to K.'s 3rd
3. Q. to K.'s 7th (mate)	

(a).

WHITE.	BLACK.
	1. K. to Kt.'s 4th
2. Q. to K. R.'s 6th (ch.)	2. K. moves
3. Q. to R.'s 4th (mate)	

No. 42.

WHITE.	BLACK.
1. B. to Q. Kt.'s 5th	1. K. to Q.'s 4th, or (a)
2. K. to K. B.'s 4th	2. Any move
3. R. or B. mates	

WHITE.	*(a).*	BLACK.
2. B. to Q.'s 7th (ch.)		1. K. to K. B.'s 4th
3. R. mates		2. K. to K.'s 4th

No. 43.

WHITE.		BLACK.
1. B. to K.'s 7th		1. K. to Q. B.'s 5th
2. Kt. to Q. Kt.'s 3rd		2. P. moves
3. Kt. mates		

No. 44.

WHITE.		BLACK.
1. R. to Q. Kt.'s sq.		1. K. to B.'s 5th, or P. moves, or *(a)*
2. R. to K. Kt.'s sq.		2. Anything
3. R. mates		
	(a).	
2. R. to Q. B.'s sq.		1. K. to Q.'s 5th
3. R. mates		2. Any move

No. 45.

WHITE.		BLACK.
1. R. from K. B.'s 5th to Q. Kt.'s 5th		1. K. moves, or *(a)*
2. R. to Q. Kt.'s 7th		2. K. moves
3. R. or Kt. mates		
	(a).	
2. R. takes Q. R.'s P.		1. R. to K.'s 7th
3. R. or Kt. mates		2. Any move

No. 46.

WHITE.		BLACK.
1. R. to Q. R.'s sq.		1. K. moves
2. B. to Q. B.'s 6th		2. K. moves
3. R. mates		

No. 47.

WHITE.		BLACK.
1. Kt. to Q. Kt.'s 4th		1. K. moves, or B. to Kt.'s 7th, or *(a)*, *(b)*
2. B. to Q.'s 6th		2. Any move
3. Q. or Kt. mates		
	(a).	
2. Kt. to Q. R.'s 6th		1. B. to B.'s 6th
3. B. mates		2. Any move
	(b).	
2. Q. to Q. B.'s 2nd		1. P. moves
3. Kt. mates		2. P. "Queens"

No. 48.

WHITE.	BLACK.
1. B. to K.'s sq.	1. B. to Q. Kt.'s 5th*
2. R. takes P.	2. Any move
3. R. or B. mates	

* If B. to Q. Kt.'s 7th, White plays B. to K. B.'s 2nd, and mates next move.

No. 49.

WHITE.	BLACK.
1. Q. to Q. Kt.'s 8th	1. K. to K. B.'s 4th, or (*a*)
2. Q. to K.'s 8th	2. K. moves
3. Q. mates	

(*a*).

	BLACK.
	1. K. to K. B.'s 2nd
2. Q. to K. Kt.'s 8th (ch.)	2. K. moves
3. Q. to K.'s 8th (mate)	

No. 50.

WHITE.	BLACK.
1. Kt. to Kt.'s 4th (ch.)	1. K. to B.'s 4th (best)
2. Q. to K.'s 4th (ch.)	2. K. or B. takes Q.
3. B. mates	

No. 51.

WHITE.	BLACK.
1. R. to K.'s 7th (ch.)	1. K. moves (best)
2. R. to K.'s 4th	2. Any move
3. R., B., or Kt. mates	

No. 52.

WHITE.	BLACK.
1. B. to Q.'s 6th (ch.).	1. K. takes B. (best)
2. P. to Q.'s 4th	2. Any move
3. R. mates	

No. 53.

WHITE.	BLACK.
1. Kt. takes Q.'s P. (ch.)	1. K. moves
2. B. to Q. B.'s 5th	2. Anywhere
3. R., B., or Kt. mate	

No. 54.

WHITE.	BLACK.
1. Kt. to Q. B.'s 5th	1. Q. to Q.'s 8th, or (*a*)
2. Q. to K.'s 4th (ch.)	2. Kt. takes Q.
3. Kt. mates	

(*a*).

	BLACK.
	1. Q. to K. Kt.'s 3rd
2. Q. takes Q.	2. P. queens
3. Kt. mates	

If Black Kt. quits K. R.'s 2nd, White Q. checks at Kt.'s 5th.

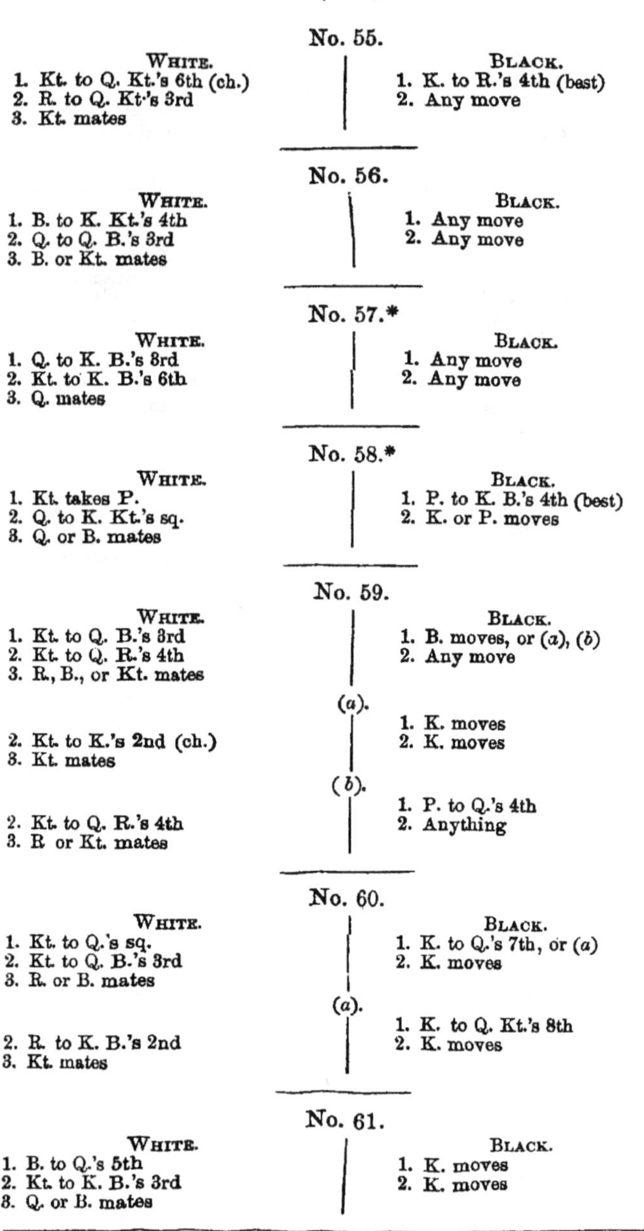

No. 55.

WHITE.	BLACK.
1. Kt. to Q. Kt.'s 6th (ch.)	1. K. to R.'s 4th (best)
2. R. to Q. Kt.'s 3rd	2. Any move
3. Kt. mates	

No. 56.

WHITE.	BLACK.
1. B. to K. Kt.'s 4th	1. Any move
2. Q. to Q. B.'s 3rd	2. Any move
3. B. or Kt. mates	

No. 57.*

WHITE.	BLACK.
1. Q. to K. B.'s 3rd	1. Any move
2. Kt. to K. B.'s 6th	2. Any move
3. Q. mates	

No. 58.*

WHITE.	BLACK.
1. Kt. takes P.	1. P. to K. B.'s 4th (best)
2. Q. to K. Kt.'s sq.	2. K. or P. moves
3. Q. or B. mates	

No. 59.

WHITE.	BLACK.
1. Kt. to Q. B.'s 3rd	1. B. moves, or (a), (b)
2. Kt. to Q. R.'s 4th	2. Any move
3. R., B., or Kt. mates	

(a).

	BLACK.
2. Kt. to K.'s 2nd (ch.)	1. K. moves
3. Kt. mates	2. K. moves

(b).

	BLACK.
2. Kt. to Q. R.'s 4th	1. P. to Q.'s 4th
3. R or Kt. mates	2. Anything

No. 60.

WHITE.	BLACK.
1. Kt. to Q.'s sq.	1. K. to Q.'s 7th, or (a)
2. Kt. to Q. B.'s 3rd	2. K. moves
3. R. or B. mates	

(a).

	BLACK.
2. R. to K. B.'s 2nd	1. K. to Q. Kt.'s 8th
3. Kt. mates	2. K. moves

No. 61.

WHITE.	BLACK.
1. B. to Q.'s 5th	1. K. moves
2. Kt. to K. B.'s 3rd	2. K. moves
3. Q. or B. mates	

* From the similarity of these positions they were called the *Twin* Problems.

No. 62.

WHITE.	BLACK.
1. Q. to K. B.'s 3rd	1. Any move
2. Kt. to K. B.'s 6th	2. Any move
3. Q. mates	

No. 63.

WHITE.	BLACK.
1. B. to Q. Kt.'s 7th	1. P. to Q. B.'s 3rd, or (a)
2. R. takes P.	2. Anywhere
3. R. or B. mates	

(a).

	1. P. takes P.
2. B. takes B. (ch.)	2. K. moves
3. B. to K. R.'s 2nd (mate)	

No. 64.

WHITE.	BLACK.
1. R. to K. Kt.'s 8th	1. K. to K. Kt.'s 4th or 5th
2. Kt. to K. R.'s 5th (ch.)	2. K. takes either Kt.
3. P. mates	

No. 65.

WHITE.	BLACK.
1. P. to Q.'s 6th	1. P. to K.'s 4th, or (a)
2. Q. to Q. R.'s 7th	2. Any move
3. Q. mates	

(a).

	1. K. to K.'s 4th*
2. Q. to Q. B.'s sq.	2. Any move
3. Q. mates	

*If K. to K. B.'s 5th, White plays Q. to Q. B.'s 5th, and mates next move.

No. 66.

WHITE.	BLACK.
1. Kt. to K.'s 4th	1. Kt. takes Kt., or R. takes R.
2. Kt. to Q.'s 3rd (dis. ch.)	or (a)
3. R. or Kt. mates	2. Anything

(a).

	1. Kt. to K. B.'s 4th
2. Kt. takes R.	2. Any move
3. R. or Kt. mates	

No. 67.

WHITE.	BLACK.
1. Kt. to Q. Kt.'s 5th (ch.)	1. K. moves (dis. ch.)
2. Kt. to Q.'s 7th	2. Anything
3. R., B., or Kt. mates	

No. 68.

WHITE.	BLACK.
1. Kt. to K.'s 3rd	1. K. to Q.'s 7th, or (a)
2. Q. to K. B.'s sq.	2. Any move
3. B. or Kt. mates	

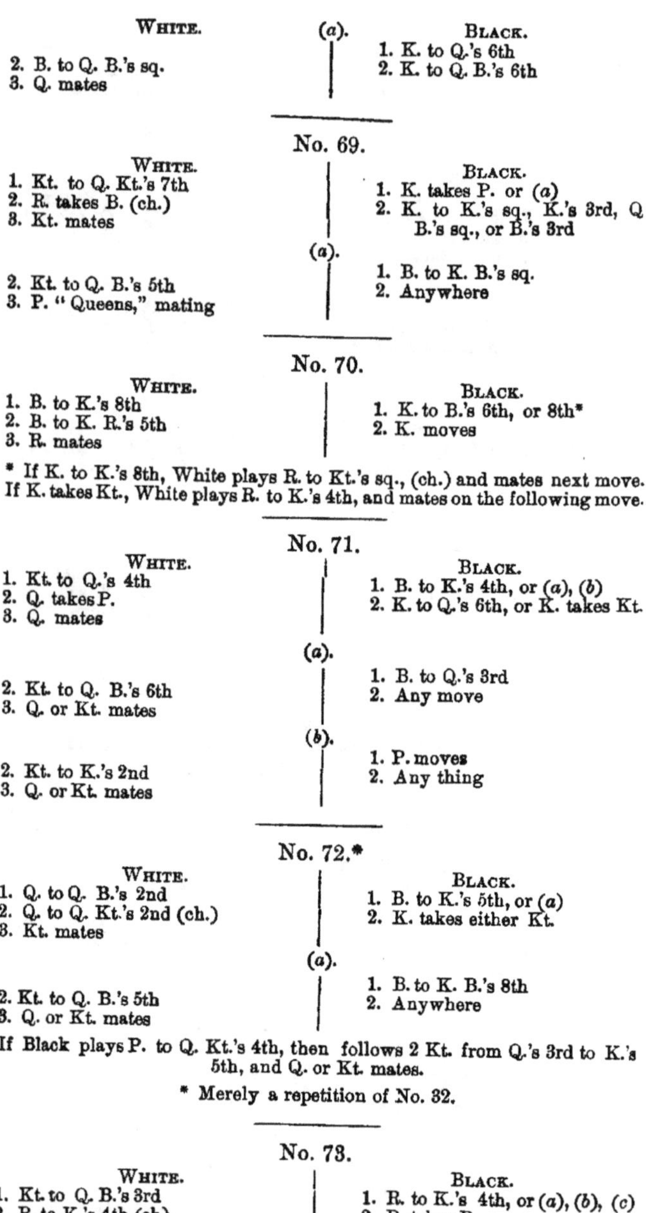

WHITE.	(*a*).	BLACK.
2. B. to Q. B.'s sq.		1. K. to Q.'s 6th
3. Q. mates		2. K. to Q. B.'s 6th

No. 69.

WHITE.		BLACK.
1. Kt. to Q. Kt.'s 7th		1. K. takes P. or (*a*)
2. R. takes B. (ch.)		2. K. to K.'s sq., K.'s 3rd, Q
3. Kt. mates		B.'s sq., or B.'s 3rd

	(*a*).	
2. Kt. to Q. B.'s 5th		1. B. to K. B.'s sq.
3. P. " Queens," mating		2. Anywhere

No. 70.

WHITE.		BLACK.
1. B. to K.'s 8th		1. K. to B.'s 6th, or 8th*
2. B. to K. R.'s 5th		2. K. moves
3. R. mates		

* If K. to K.'s 8th, White plays R. to Kt.'s sq., (ch.) and mates next move.
If K. takes Kt., White plays R. to K.'s 4th, and mates on the following move.

No. 71.

WHITE.		BLACK.
1. Kt. to Q.'s 4th		1. B. to K.'s 4th, or (*a*), (*b*)
2. Q. takes P.		2. K. to Q.'s 6th, or K. takes Kt.
3. Q. mates		

	(*a*).	
2. Kt. to Q. B.'s 6th		1. B. to Q.'s 3rd
3. Q. or Kt. mates		2. Any move

	(*b*).	
2. Kt. to K.'s 2nd		1. P. moves
3. Q. or Kt. mates		2. Any thing

No. 72.*

WHITE.		BLACK.
1. Q. to Q. B.'s 2nd		1. B. to K.'s 5th, or (*a*)
2. Q. to Q. Kt.'s 2nd (ch.)		2. K. takes either Kt.
3. Kt. mates		

	(*a*).	
2. Kt. to Q. B.'s 5th		1. B. to K. B.'s 8th
3. Q. or Kt. mates		2. Anywhere

If Black plays P. to Q. Kt.'s 4th, then follows 2 Kt. from Q.'s 3rd to K.'s
5th, and Q. or Kt. mates.

* Merely a repetition of No. 32.

No. 73.

WHITE.		BLACK.
1. Kt. to Q. B.'s 3rd		1. R. to K.'s 4th, or (*a*), (*b*), (*c*)
2. R. to K.'s 4th (ch).		2. R. takes R.
3. Kt. takes Kt., (mate)		

WHITE.	*(a).*	**BLACK.**
		1. Kt. from K.'s sq. to Q. B.'s 2nd
2. Kt. takes R.		2. Any move
3. R. or Kt. mates		
	(b).	
		1. Kt. to Q. Kt.'s 3rd
2. B. takes P.		2. Any move
3. R. or Kt. mates		
	(c).	
		1. Kt. takes Kt.
2. Kt. to Q. Kt.'s 4th		2. Any move
3. Kt. mates		

No. 74.

WHITE.	**BLACK.**
1. B. to Q.'s 5th	1. K. moves
2. R. takes P.	2. K. moves
3. B. mates	

No. 75.

WHITE.		**BLACK.**
1. Kt. to Q. B.'s 4th		1. B. takes Kt., or *(a), (b)*
2. P. to Q.'s 4th		2. Any move
3. Kt. mates		
	(a).	
		1. Kt. to Q.'s 3rd
2. Kt. to K. B.'s 6th (ch.)		2. K. takes Kt.
3. B. mates		
	(b).	
		1. Kt. to K. Kt.'s 4th
2. Kt. to K.'s 3rd (ch.)		2. K. moves
3. Kt. mates		

No. 76.

WHITE.		**BLACK.**
1. Kt. takes Kt.'s P.		1. B. to K.'s 5th, or *(a,) (b)*
2. Q. to K. R.'s 2nd (ch.)		2. K. takes Kt.
3. Kt. mates		
	(a).	
		1. B. takes Kt.
2. Kt. to K. Kt.'s 5th (ch.)		2. Any move
3. Q. or Kt. mates		
	(b).	
		1. Kt. to K.'s 8th
2. B. takes P. (ch.)		2. K. moves
3. Kt. takes Kt. mate		

No. 77.

WHITE.		**BLACK.**
1. Kt. to Q. B.'s 3rd		1. R. to K.'s 4th, or *(a), (b), (c)*
2. R. to K.'s 4th (ch.)		R. takes R.
3. Kt. mates		
	(a).	
		1. Kt. takes Kt.
2. Kt. to Q. Kt.'s 4th		2. Any move
3. Kt. mates		

WHITE.	(b).	BLACK.
		1. Kt. to Q. Kt.'s 3rd.
2. B. takes P.		2. Any move
3. R. or Kt. mates		
	(c).	
		1. Kt. to Q. B.'s 2nd
2. Kt. takes R.		2. Any move
3. R. or Kt. mates		

A repetition of No. 73.

No. 78.

WHITE.	BLACK.
1. B. to Q. B.'s 7th	1. B. to K. B.'s sq.*
2. K. takes B.	2. K. moves
3. R. to Q. B.'s 5th, (dis. ch., mate)	

* If B. to K. R.'s 5th, White R. is moved to K. Kt.'s 5th, (ch.), and Q.'s B. mates next move.

No. 79.

WHITE.	BLACK.
1. Kt. to K.'s 8th	1. K. moves
2. Kt. to Q.'s 6th	2. K. to K.'s 6th, or Q. B.'s 6th
3. Kt. mates	

No. 80.

WHITE.	BLACK.
1. Kt. to K. B.'s 8th	1. Any move
2. Kt. to K.'s 6th	2. Any move
3. Kt. mates	

No. 81.

WHITE.	BLACK.
1. Q. to Q.'s 8th	1. P. takes Kt. (best)*
2. Kt. to K.'s sq.	2. Any thing
3. Q. mates	

* Black has a variety of defences, but the mate will still be effected in three moves.

No. 82.

WHITE.	BLACK.
1. Kt. to Q. Kt.'s 5th.	1. P. to Q. B.'s 4th, or (a)
2. Kt. takes Q.'s P.	2. Any move
3. B., Kt., or P. mates	
	(a).
	1. R. to Q.'s 2nd
2. Kt. to Q. R.'s 7th	2. Any move
3. B., Kt., or P. mates	

No. 83.

WHITE.	BLACK.
1. B. to K. Kt.'s 3rd	1. K moves
2. B. to K. R.'s 4th	2. K. moves
3. B. mates	

No. 84.

WHITE.	BLACK.
1. B. to Q.'s 5th	1. K. to Q. B.'s 4th, or (a)
2. B. to Q. B.'s 7th	2. K. moves
3. B. mates	

(a).

	1. K. to K.'s 6th
2. B. to K. Kt.'s 2nd	2. Any move
3. R. or B. mates	

No. 85.

WHITE.	BLACK.
1. B. to Q. Kt.'s 4th	1. P. to Q. B.'s 4th (best)
2. Q. to K.'s 4th	2. Any move
3. Q. mates	

. No. 86.

WHITE.	BLACK.
1. R. to K. B.'s 6th	1. K. to Q.'s 5th, or (a)
2. B. to K. B.'s 3rd	2. K. moves
3. R. or B. mates	

(a).

	1. K. to K.'s 7th
2. B. to Q.'s 2nd	2. P. moves
3. B. to Q. B.'s 4th, (mate)	

No. 87.

WHITE.	BLACK.
1. Kt. to K. B.'s 2nd	1. K. to Q.'s 4th
2. Kt. to Q.'s 3rd	2. K. moves
3. B. mates	

No. 88.

WHITE.	BLACK.
1. Kt. to K. Kt.'s 6th	1. P. takes Kt. at K.'s 3rd
2. Kt. K. B.'s 4th (dis. ch.)	2. K. moves
K. mates	

No. 89.

WHITE.	BLACK.
1. P. to Q. B.'s 3rd	1. Kt. takes R., or (a)
2. Kt. to K. R.'s 3rd	2. Any move
3. Kt. mates	

(a).

	1. Kt. checks
2. K. to K.'s 7th	2. Any move
3. R. to K.'s 3rd mating	

No. 90.

WHITE.	BLACK.
1. Kt. to Kt.'s sq.	1. K. moves
2. Kt. to K. R.'s 3rd	2. Any move
3. Kt. or B. mates	

No. 91.

WHITE.
1. Kt. to K. Kt.'s 2nd
2. Kt. to K.'s 3rd
3. Kt. or B. mates

BLACK.
1. K. moves
2. Anywhere

No. 92.

WHITE.
1. Kt to K. B.'s 5th
2. Kt. takes P.
3. R., B., or Kt. mates

BLACK.
1. B. to K. R.'s 5th or (a), (b)
2. Any move

(a).

2. Kt. to K. Kt.'s 7th
3. R. or Kt. mates

1. Kt. to K. Kt.'s 5th
2. Any move

(b).

2. Kt. to K. R.'s 6th
3. R. mates

1. Kt. to Q.'s 8th
2. Any move

No. 93.

WHITE.
1. Q. to Q.'s sq.
2. Q. to K. Kt.'s 4th
3. Q. mates

BLACK.
1. K. to Q.'s 4th, or (a)
2. K. takes P.

(a).

2. Q. to K. Kt.'s 4th (ch.)
3. Q. mates

1. K. to B.'s 4th
2. K. moves

No. 94.

WHITE.
1. Kt. to K.'s 6th
2. Kt. to Q. B.'s 5th
3. Kt. mates

BLACK.
1. Any move
2. Any move

No. 95.

WHITE.
1. R. takes Kt. (ch.)
2. B. to K. B.'s 6th
3. Q. mates

BLACK.
1. K. takes R., or (a), (b)
2. Anything

(a).

2. B. to Q.'s 4th (dble. ch.)
2. R. mates

1. Kt. takes R.
2. K. takes B.

(b).

2. B. to Q.'s 4th (dble. ch.)
3. Q. mate

1. Q., R., B., or P. takes R.
2. K. takes B.

No. 96.

WHITE.
1. B. to Q. Kt.'s 8th
2. R. to Q. B.'s 7th
3. R. to Q. B.'s 4th, (dis. ch., mate)

BLACK.
1. P. moves, or (a), (b)
2. K. moves

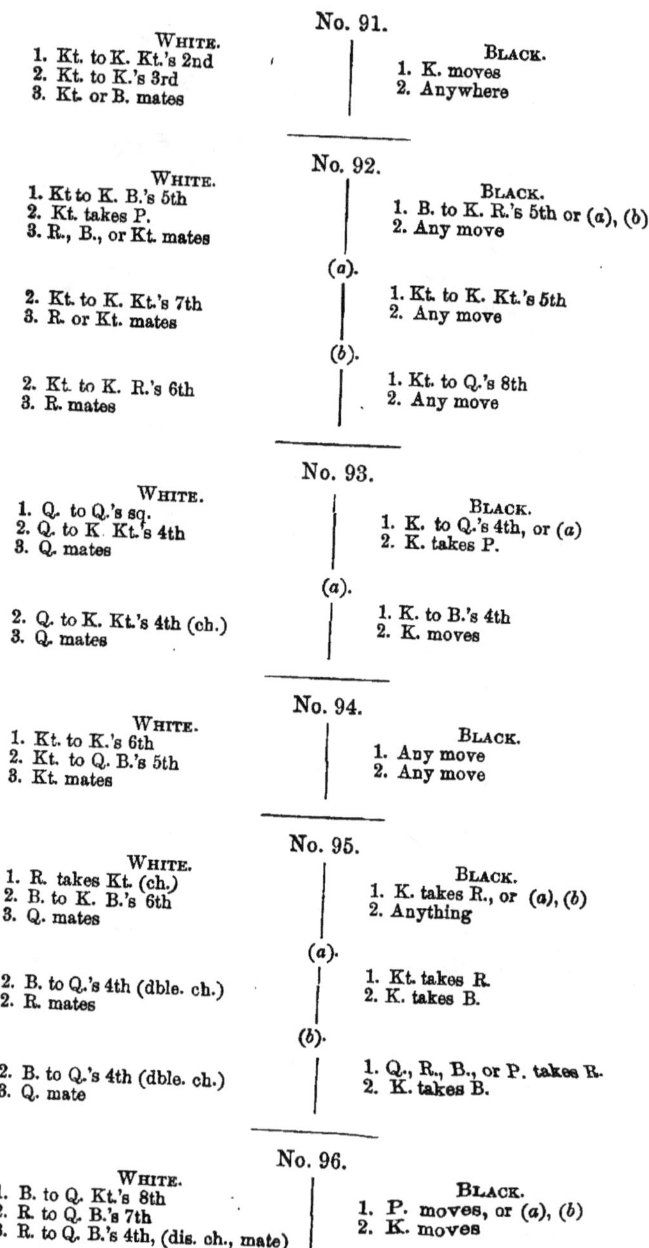

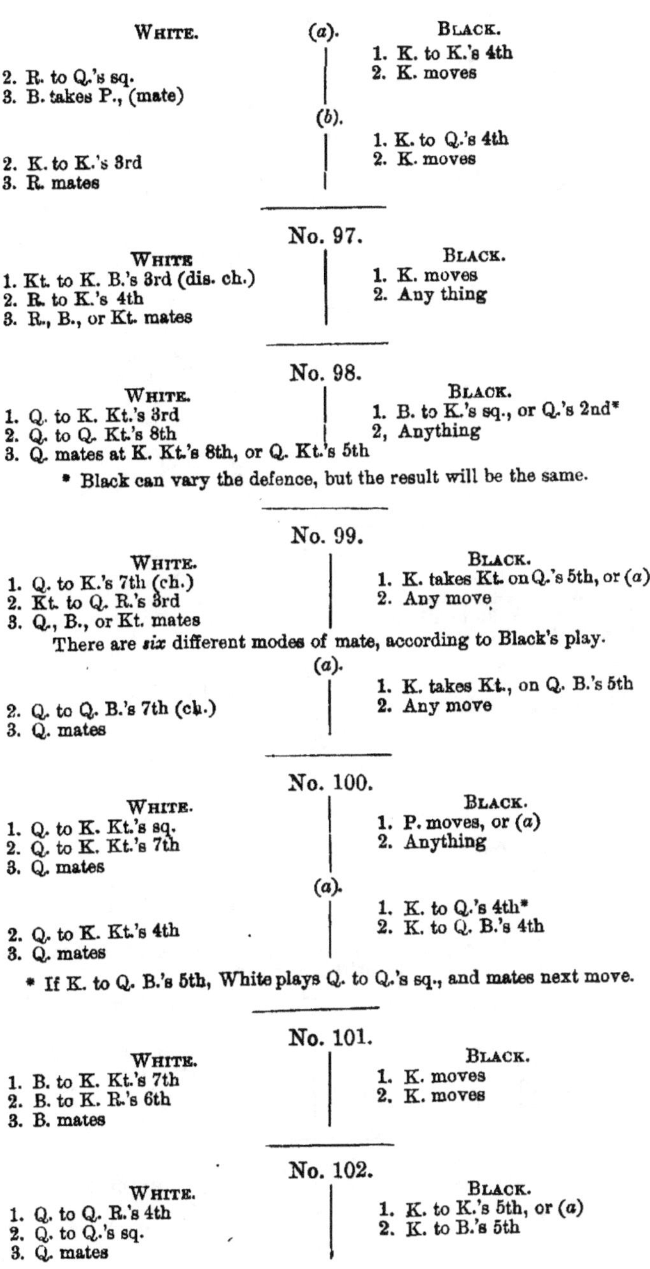

WHITE.	(a).	BLACK.
		1. K. to K.'s 4th
2. R. to Q.'s sq.		2. K. moves
3. B. takes P., (mate)		
	(b).	
		1. K. to Q.'s 4th
2. K. to K.'s 3rd		2. K. moves
3. R. mates		

No. 97.

WHITE	BLACK.
1. Kt. to K. B.'s 3rd (dis. ch.)	1. K. moves
2. R. to K.'s 4th	2. Any thing
3. R., B., or Kt. mates	

No. 98.

WHITE.	BLACK.
1. Q. to K. Kt.'s 3rd	1. B. to K.'s sq., or Q.'s 2nd*
2. Q. to Q. Kt.'s 8th	2, Anything
3. Q. mates at K. Kt.'s 8th, or Q. Kt.'s 5th	

* Black can vary the defence, but the result will be the same.

No. 99.

WHITE.	BLACK.
1. Q. to K.'s 7th (ch.)	1. K. takes Kt. on Q.'s 5th, or (a)
2. Kt. to Q. R.'s 3rd	2. Any move
3. Q., B., or Kt. mates	

There are *six* different modes of mate, according to Black's play.

(a).	
	1. K. takes Kt., on Q. B.'s 5th
2. Q. to Q. B.'s 7th (ch.)	2. Any move
3. Q. mates	

No. 100.

WHITE.	BLACK.
1. Q. to K. Kt.'s sq.	1. P. moves, or (a)
2. Q. to K. Kt.'s 7th	2. Anything
3. Q. mates	

(a).	
	1. K. to Q.'s 4th*
2. Q. to K. Kt.'s 4th	2. K. to Q. B.'s 4th
3. Q. mates	

* If K. to Q. B.'s 5th, White plays Q. to Q.'s sq., and mates next move.

No. 101.

WHITE.	BLACK.
1. B. to K. Kt.'s 7th	1. K. moves
2. B. to K. R.'s 6th	2. K. moves
3. B. mates	

No. 102.

WHITE.	BLACK.
1. Q. to Q. R.'s 4th	1. K. to K.'s 5th, or (a)
2. Q. to Q.'s sq.	2. K. to B.'s 5th
3. Q. mates	

WHITE.	(a).	BLACK.
2. Q. to Q.'s sq. (ch.)		1. K. to K.'s 7th
3. Kt. to K. B.'s (dis. ch. and mate)		2. K. to K. B.'s 7th

No. 103.

WHITE.		BLACK.
1. B. to K. Kt.'s 8th		1. Kt. to K. B.'s sq. (best)
2. R. to K.'s 6th		2. Kt. takes R., or (a)
3. B. mates		
	(a).	
3. Kt. mates		2. Kt. to Kt.'s 3rd

No. 104.

WHITE.		BLACK.
1. R. to K. R.'s 4th		1. P. to Q. Kt.'s 5th, or (a)
2. Kt. to Q.'s 5th (ch.)		2. Any move
3. R. or Kt. mates		
	(a).	
2. R. checks		1. R. takes Kt.
3. R. takes R. (mate)		2. R. to K. B.'s 6th

No. 105.

WHITE.		BLACK.
1. R. to K. B.'s 6th (ch).		1. K. to Q.'s 4th *
2. R. at K. B.'s 6th to K.'s 6th		2. Q. takes R. or (a), (b), (c), (d)
3. R. to Q.'s 6th (mate)		
	(a)	
3. P. takes Kt. (mate)		2. Kt. takes Kt.
	(b).	
3. Kt. mates		2. Kt. takes P.
	(c).	
3. Kt. takes B. (mate)		2. B. checks
	(d).	
3. R. mates		2. R. to Q. B.'s 3rd

* If Black play K. to Q.'s 2nd, White R. checks at Q.'s 6th, and the other
R. mates next moves

No. 106.

WHITE.		BLACK.
1. B. to K.'s 6th		1. K. moves (best)
2. B. to Q.'s 4th		2. Any move
3. Mate accordingly		

No. 107.

WHITE.		BLACK.
1. Q. to Q. B.'s 4th		1. K. to B.'s 5th, or (a)
2. Kt. takes P.		2. K. takes either Kt.
3. Q. mates		

WHITE.	(a).	BLACK.
		1. P. to K.'s 6th
2. Q. to K.'s 6th		2. Any move
3. Q. mates		

No. 108.

WHITE.	BLACK.
1. Q. to K. Kt.'s 3rd (ch.)	1. K. takes Kt. on Q.'s 5th, or (a)
2. Kt. to Q. B.'s 7th	2. Any move
3. Q. or Kt. mates	

(a).

	1. K. takes Kt. on Q.'s 4th
2. Q. to K. Kt.'s 5th (ch.)	2. K. moves
3. Q. to Q. B.'s 5th (mate)	

This position is an amendment of a Problem by Mr. Grimshaw, of Whitby.

No. 109.

WHITE.	BLACK.
1. Kt. to K. R.'s 6th	1. K. moves, or (a)
2. Kt. to K. B.'s 7th	2. Any move
3. Kt. mates	

(a).

	1. B. to Q. B.'s 5th
2. Kt. to K. Kt.'s 4th	2. Any move
3. Q. mates	

No. 110.

WHITE.	BLACK.
1. B. to K. Kt.'s 3rd	1. R. to K. B.'s 2nd, or (a)
2. Kt. to K. B.'s 4th (dis. ch.)	2. K. moves
3. R. or Kt. mates	

(a).

	1. P. to Q. Kt.'s 6th*
2. Kt. to K. B.'s 4th (ch.)	2. K. to Q. B.'s 6th
3. B. to K.'s sq. mate	

* If K. to Q. B.'s 4th, White plays Kt. to Q. B.'s 7th, and mates next move.

No. 111.

WHITE.	BLACK.
1. Kt. to K. B.'s 5th	1. K. takes P., or (a)
2. R. to Q. Kt.'s 5th ch.	2. K. moves
3. Kt. mates	

(a).

	1. Any other move
2. Kt. to K.'s 3rd	2. Any move
3. Kt. to Q.'s 3rd (mate)	

No. 112.

WHITE.	BLACK.
1. B. to Q. R.'s 6th	1. K. moves
2. R. to Q. B.'s 4th	2. Kt. moves
3. R. or B. mates	

No. 113.

WHITE.	BLACK.
1. Q. to Q. B.'s sq.	1. B. to K.'s 6th (ch.)*
2. Q. takes B. (ch.)	2. Kt. takes Q
3. Kt. mates	

* Black has a variety of defences. If he play—1. B. to Q. Kt.'s 3rd, or, 1. R. to Q. R.'s 4th, White plays, 2. Kt. to K.'s 5th (dis. ch.), and mates next move. If he play—1. B. to Q. Kt.'s 6th, White plays, 2. Kt. to Q.'s 2nd. If he play—1. B. to Q. Kt.'s 8th, or, 1. P. to Q. Kt.'s 6th, White answers with 2. Q. to Q. B.'s 4th (ch.); and lastly, if 1. B to Q. B.'s 4th, or, 1. B. to K. Kt.'s 8th, White's reply is, 2. Q. takes B., in each case mating on the following move.

No. 114.

WHITE.	BLACK.
1. Q. to Q. B.'s 8th	1. K. to K.'s 4th, or (a), (b)
2. Q. to Q. B.'s sq.	2. Any move
3. Q. mates	

(a).

	1. K. to B.'s 5th
2. Q. to Q. B.'s 5th	2. Any move
3. Q. mates	

(b).

	1. K. to Kt.'s 3rd
2. Q. to K. Kt.'s 8th (ch.)	2. Any move
3. Q. mates	

No. 115.

WHITE.	BLACK.
1. Kt. to K. Kt.'s 7th	1. K. moves
2. Kt. to K.'s 8th	2. K. moves
3. B. or Kt. mates	

No. 116.

WHITE.	BLACK.
1. Kt. to Q. Kt.'s 4th (ch.)	1. K. to Q. B.'s 4th (best)
2. Q. to Q.'s 4th (ch.)	2. K. or B. takes Q.
3. B. mates	

This Problem is only another version of No. 50.

No. 117.

WHITE.	BLACK.
1. B. to Q. Kt.'s sq.	1. Kt. checks, or (a)
2. K. takes P.	2. Any move
3. Kt., R., or B. mates	

(a).

	1. Kt. to Q.'s 7th
2. B. takes P.	2. Any move
3. R or Kt. mates	

No. 118.

WHITE.	BLACK.
1. B. to K. R.'s 3rd (dis. ch.)	1. K. to Q. B.'s 5th (best)
2. R. takes R.	2. K. or B. takes either R.
3. B. mates	

No. 119.

WHITE.	BLACK.
1. Kt. from K.'s 8th to Q.'s 6th	1. B. to Q. B.'s 2nd, or R.'s 2nd, or (a)
2. Kt. to Q. Kt.'s 7th	
3. Kt. mates	2. Any move

(a).

WHITE.	BLACK.
	1. Kt. moves
2. Kt. to K. B.'s 5th	2. Anything
3. Kt. mates	

No. 120.

WHITE.	BLACK.
1. Kt. to Q.'s 3rd	1. Kt. to Q. B.'s 3rd *
2. Kt. to Q. Kt.'s 2nd	2. Kt. takes R.
3. B. to K.'s 5th (mate)	

* If Black move B. to K. Kt.'s 6th, or R. to K.'s square, White plays Kt. to Q. B.'s square, and mates next move.

No. 121.

WHITE.	BLACK.
1. Q. to K. B.'s 7th	1. R. to Q. B.'s 8th, or K. moves
2. Kt. to Q. B.'s 6th	
3. Q. or R. mates	2. Any move

No. 122.

WHITE.	BLACK.
1. Q. to K.'s 3rd	1. Kt. takes Q., or (a), (b), (c)
2. R. checks	2. K. takes Kt.
3. B. to Q.'s 3rd (mating)	

(a).

WHITE.	BLACK.
	1. B. takes R.
2. Q. to Q.'s 3rd (ch.)	2. K. to K.'s 3rd
3. Q. to Q.'s 7th (mate)	

(b).

WHITE.	BLACK.
	1. R. to K.'s 3rd
2. Q. to Q.'s 3rd (ch.)	2. K. to K.'s 4th
3. R. to K. Kt.'s 5th (mate)	

(c).

WHITE.	BLACK.
	1. R. to K. B.'s 4th, or K. R's 4th
2. Kt. to Q. B.'s 3rd (ch.)	2. Kt. takes Kt.
3. B. to Q. B.'s 6th (mate)	

No. 123.

WHITE.	BLACK.
1. R. takes Kt.	1. Anything
2. R. to Q.'s 8th	2. Anything
3. B. mates	

No. 124.

WHITE.	BLACK.
1. Q. to Q. R.'s sq.	1. K. to K. B.'s 5th (best)
2. Q. to Q. R.'s 6th	2. K. moves
3. Q. mates	

No. 125.

WHITE.	BLACK.
1. Kt. to Q. R.'s 6th	1. K. moves
2. Kt. to Q. B.'s 5th	2. K. to any of the four squares
3. Kt. or B. mates	at command

No. 126.

WHITE.	BLACK.
1. Kt. to K.'s 6th	1. B. to Q. B.'s 8th, or (a)
2. Kt. to Q.'s 4th	2. Any move
3. R. or Kt. mates	

(a).

2. K. to Q. B's 4th	1. P. takes Kt. (ch.)
3. Mates accordingly	2. Any move

No. 127.

WHITE.	BLACK.
1. Kt. to Q. Kt.'s 2nd	1. K. moves
2. Kt. to Q. R.'s 4th	2. K. moves
3. B. or Kt. mates	

No. 128.

WHITE.	BLACK.
1. B. to K. Kt.'s 4th	1. Kt. to K.'s 5th, or (a)
2. B. to K.'s 6th	2. Kt. takes R. *
3. K. to Q.'s 4th (dis. ch., mate)	

(a).

2. B. takes Kt.	1. Kt. to K. B.'s 4th
3. Mates accordingly	2. Anything

* Black can vary this move, but if he does the result will be the same.

No. 129.

WHITE.	BLACK.
1. B. to Q. B.'s 3rd	1. K. to Q.'s 4th, or (a)
2. B. to K.'s 5th	2. Any move
3. Q., R., or B. mate	

(a).

2. B. to K.'s 6th	1. R. takes R. ; K. takes B., or Kt. to K.'s 2nd
3. Q. mates	2. B. or Kt. covers

No. 130.

WHITE.	BLACK.
1. P. to Q. B.'s 5th	1. R. takes Q.'s B. P. (a)
2. B. to K. B.'s 5th (ch.)	2. Any move
3. Q. mates	

(a).

	1. B. to K.'s 6th
2. Q. to K.'s 2nd	2. Any move
3. Q. mates	

No. 131.

WHITE.	BLACK.
1. Kt. to Q. B.'s 5th	1. K. takes P., or (a)
2. R. to K. Kt.'s 5th (ch.)	2. K. moves
3. Kt. mates	

(a).

	1. K. to K. B.'s 5th ; P. takes
2. Kt. to Q.'s 3rd	P., or P. to B.'s 7th
3. P. mates	2. K. moves

No. 132.*

WHITE.	BLACK.
1. Q. to Q. R.'s 7th	1. Any move
2. Kt. to K.'s 6th	2. Any move
3. Q. or B. mates	

* A repetition only of No. 39.

No. 133.

WHITE.	BLACK.
1. R. to Q. Kt.'s 2nd	1. K. moves
2. B. to K. Kt.'s 3rd	2. K. to Q.'s 5th
3. B. to Q.'s 6th	3. K. moves
4. B. mates	

No. 134.

WHITE.	BLACK.
1. B. to Q. R.'s 3rd	1. P. moves
2. P. moves	2. P. moves
3. B. to Q. B.'s sq.	3. K. to B.'s 5th
4. R. mates	

No. 135.

WHITE.	BLACK.
1. Kt. to Q.'s sq.	1. P. to K.'s 5th (best)
2. Kt. to Q. B.'s 3rd	2. Anything
3. Kt. to K.'s 2nd, or 4th	3. Anything
4. Kt. mates	

No. 136.

WHITE.	BLACK.
1. B. to K. Kt.'s 7th	1.
2. P. to Q.'s 4th	2. } All forced
3. B. to K. R.'s 6th	3.
4. Kt. mates	

No. 137.

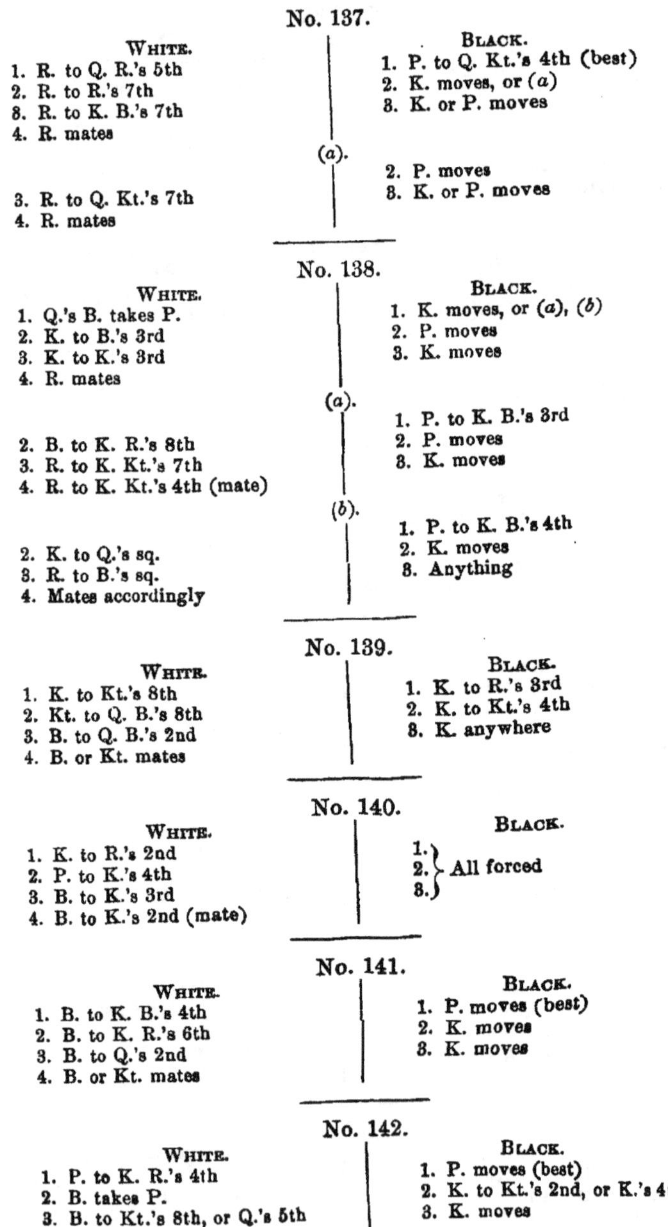

WHITE.	BLACK.
1. R. to Q. R.'s 5th	1. P. to Q. Kt.'s 4th (best)
2. R. to R.'s 7th	2. K. moves, or (*a*)
3. R. to K. B.'s 7th	3. K. or P. moves
4. R. mates	

(*a*).

	2. P. moves
3. R. to Q. Kt.'s 7th	3. K. or P. moves
4. R. mates	

No. 138.

WHITE.	BLACK.
1. Q.'s B. takes P.	1. K. moves, or (*a*), (*b*)
2. K. to B.'s 3rd	2. P. moves
3. K. to K.'s 3rd	3. K. moves
4. R. mates	

(*a*).

2. B. to K. R.'s 8th	1. P. to K. B.'s 3rd
3. R. to K. Kt.'s 7th	2. P. moves
4. R. to K. Kt.'s 4th (mate)	3. K. moves

(*b*).

2. K. to Q.'s sq.	1. P. to K. B.'s 4th
3. R. to B.'s sq.	2. K. moves
4. Mates accordingly	3. Anything

No. 139.

WHITE.	BLACK.
1. K. to Kt.'s 8th	1. K. to R.'s 3rd
2. Kt. to Q. B.'s 8th	2. K. to Kt.'s 4th
3. B. to Q. B.'s 2nd	3. K. anywhere
4. B. or Kt. mates	

No. 140.

WHITE.	BLACK.
1. K. to R.'s 2nd	1.
2. P. to K.'s 4th	2. } All forced
3. B. to K.'s 3rd	3.
4. B. to K.'s 2nd (mate)	

No. 141.

WHITE.	BLACK.
1. B. to K. B.'s 4th	1. P. moves (best)
2. B. to K. R.'s 6th	2. K. moves
3. B. to Q.'s 2nd	3. K. moves
4. B. or Kt. mates	

No. 142.

WHITE.	BLACK.
1. P. to K. R.'s 4th	1. P. moves (best)
2. B. takes P.	2. K. to Kt.'s 2nd, or K.'s 4th
3. B. to Kt.'s 8th, or Q.'s 5th	3. K. moves
4. B. mates	

No. 143.

WHITE.	BLACK.
1. B. to K.'s 8th	1. Any move
2. Kt. to K.'s 5th	2. Any move
3. Kt. to Q.'s 3rd	3. Any move
4. B. or Kt. mates	

No. 144.

WHITE.	BLACK.
1. B. to K. B.'s 7th	1. P. to K. B.'s 4th, or (a), (b)
2. B. to K.'s 6th	2. P. moves
3. R. to K. Kt.'s 2nd	3. K. or P. moves
4. B. or R. mates	

(a).

	1. P. to K.'s 3rd
2. B. to K.'s 8th	2. K. moves
3. R. takes P.	3. Anything
4. B. mates	

(b).

	1. P. to K.'s 4th
2. B. to K.'s 8th	2. K. to Q.'s 4th (best)
3. R. takes B.'s P.	3. K. or P. moves
4. R. or B. mates	

No. 145.

WHITE.	BLACK.
1. Kt. to K.'s 4th	1. K. to Q.'s 4th
2. P. to K.'s 3rd	2. P. takes P.
3. P. to K. B.'s 4th	3. K. or P. moves
4. R. mates	

No. 146.

WHITE.	BLACK.
1. B. to K. B.'s sq.	1. Kt. to K.'s 3rd (ch.)
2. K. to Q. B.'s 8th	2. Kt. moves
3. B. to K. Kt.'s 2nd, or Q. B.'s 4th	3. Anything
4. B. mates	

No. 147.

WHITE.	BLACK.
1. R. to Q.'s 6th	1. P. moves
2. R. to Q. Kt.'s 6th	2. K. moves (best)
3. B. to Q. Kt.'s 4th	3. K. or P. moves
4. R. or B. mates	

No. 148.

WHITE.	BLACK.
1. Q.'s Kt. takes P. (dis. ch.)	1. R. interposes
2. R. to K. B.'s 6th	2. Kt. takes R., or (a)
3. Kt. to Q. Kt.'s 6th	3. Anywhere
4. Kt. mates	

WHITE. (a). BLACK.

WHITE.	BLACK.
3. K. to K.'s 2nd	2. Kt. checks
4. B. mates	3. Any move

No. 149.

WHITE.	BLACK.
1. Kt. to Q.'s 5th (dis. ch.)	1. K. to Q.'s 5th (best)
2. R. takes B.	2. Kt. to Q. B.'s 8th, or (a), (b)
3. B. to Q. Kt.'s 4th	3. Any move.
4. Kt. mates	

(a).

WHITE.	BLACK.
3. Kt. to Q. B.'s 7th (dis. ch.)	2. Kt. to Q. B.'s 6th
4. Kt. mates	3. Kt. covers

(b).

WHITE.	BLACK.
3. Kt. to Q. Kt.'s 4th (dis. ch.)	2. P. moves
4. R. to Q.'s 3rd or 5th (mate)	3. K. moves.

No. 150.

WHITE.	BLACK.
1. B. to K. B.'s 5th	1. K. to K. B.'s 7th, or (a)
2. K. to K. B.'s 4th	2. K. to K.'s 7th or Kt.'s 7th
3. K. to K.'s 3rd, or K. Kt.'s 3rd	3. K. or B. moves
4. R. mates	

(a).

WHITE.	BLACK.
2. K. to B.'s 4th	1. B. to R.'s 7th
3. R. takes P. (ch.)	2. K. to B.'s 7th
4. B. mates	3. K. moves

No. 151.

WHITE.	BLACK.
1. Kt. to Q.'s 3rd	1. K. moves
2. B. to Q.'s 8th	2. K. moves
3. B. to Q. Kt.'s 6th	3. K. moves
4. Kt. mates	

No. 152.

WHITE.	BLACK.
1. Kt. to Q.'s 5th (dis. ch.)	1. K. to Q.'s 5th, or (a)
2. R. to Q.'s 6th	2. Kt. to Q. B.'s 6th
3. Kt. to Q. B.'s 7th (dis. ch.)	3. Kt. to Q.'s 4th
4. Kt. mates	

(a).

WHITE.	BLACK.
2. R. to Q. Kt.'s 6th (ch.)	1. K. to Q. Kt.'s 4th
3. B. to Q.'s 6th	2. K. moves
4. B. mates	3. Kt. moves

This is only another version of No. 149.

No. 153.

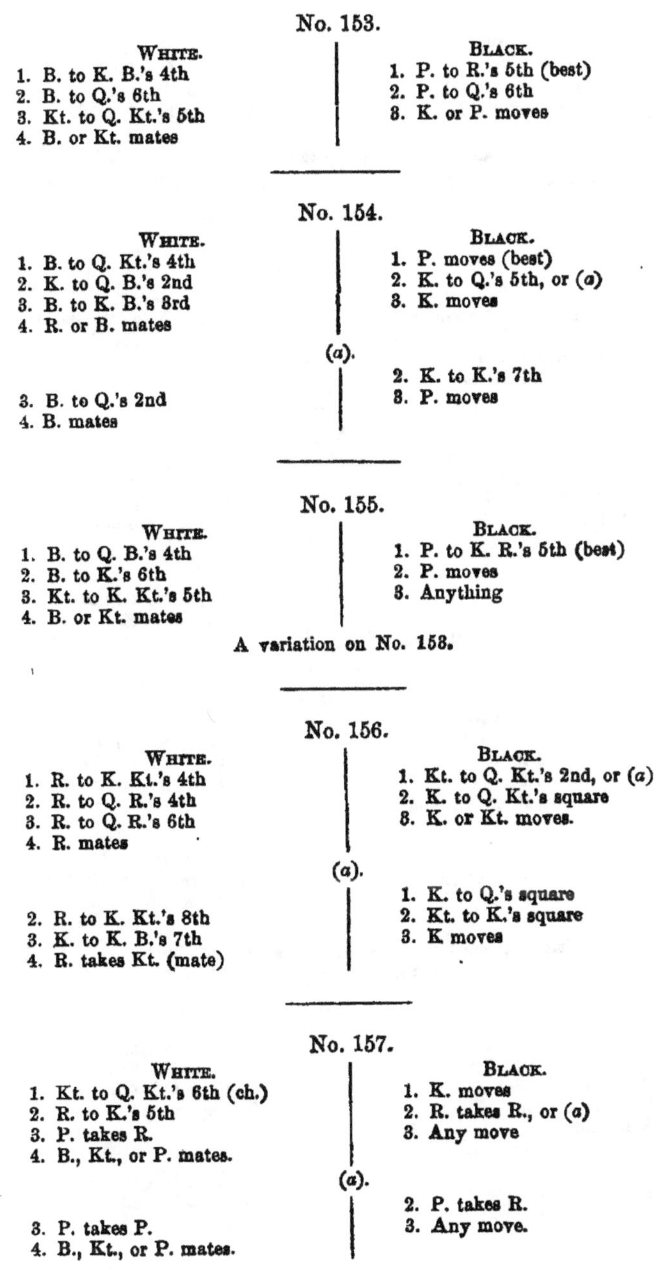

WHITE.	BLACK.
1. B. to K. B.'s 4th	1. P. to R.'s 5th (best)
2. B. to Q.'s 6th	2. P. to Q.'s 6th
3. Kt. to Q. Kt.'s 5th	3. K. or P. moves
4. B. or Kt. mates	

No. 154.

WHITE.	BLACK.
1. B. to Q. Kt.'s 4th	1. P. moves (best)
2. K. to Q. B.'s 2nd	2. K. to Q.'s 5th, or (a)
3. B. to K. B.'s 3rd	3. K. moves
4. R. or B. mates	

(a).

	BLACK.
	2. K. to K.'s 7th
3. B. to Q.'s 2nd	3. P. moves
4. B. mates	

No. 155.

WHITE.	BLACK.
1. B. to Q. B.'s 4th	1. P. to K. R.'s 5th (best)
2. B. to K.'s 6th	2. P. moves
3. Kt. to K. Kt.'s 5th	3. Anything
4. B. or Kt. mates	

A variation on No. 153.

No. 156.

WHITE.	BLACK.
1. R. to K. Kt.'s 4th	1. Kt. to Q. Kt.'s 2nd, or (a)
2. R. to Q. R.'s 4th	2. K. to Q. Kt.'s square
3. R. to Q. R.'s 6th	3. K. or Kt. moves.
4. R. mates	

(a).

WHITE.	BLACK.
	1. K. to Q.'s square
2. R. to K. Kt.'s 8th	2. Kt. to K.'s square
3. K. to K. B.'s 7th	3. K moves
4. R. takes Kt. (mate)	

No. 157.

WHITE.	BLACK.
1. Kt. to Q. Kt.'s 6th (ch.)	1. K. moves
2. R. to K.'s 5th	2. R. takes R., or (a)
3. P. takes R.	3. Any move
4. B., Kt., or P. mates.	

(a).

WHITE.	BLACK.
	2. P. takes R.
3. P. takes P.	3. Any move.
4. B., Kt., or P. mates.	

No. 158.

WHITE.	BLACK.
1. B. to Q.'s 8th	1. K. to B.'s 5th*
2. Kt. to Q.'s 5th (ch.)	2. K. to B.'s 4th
3. Kt. to K.'s 3rd (ch.)	3. K. to B.'s 5th (a)
4. B. mates	

* If any other move, white still plays Kt. to Q.'s 5th.

(a) If Black play K. to K.'s 3rd, White plays B. to K. R.'s 3rd (mate).

A variation on No. 143.

No. 159.

WHITE.	BLACK.
1. R. from Q. B.'s 7th to B.'s 6th	1. Kt. to K.'s 4th (best)
2. R. to K.'s 6th	2. K. moves (best)
3. R. on K.'s 6th takes Kt.	3. Any move.
4. R. or Kt. mates	

No. 160.

WHITE.	BLACK.
1. P. to Q. B.'s 4th (ch.)	1. Kt. takes P.
2. R. to K.'s 4th	2. Kt. takes R., or (a)
3. Kt. takes K. B.'s P.	3. Either Kt. moves.
4. Kt. mates.	

(a).

WHITE.	BLACK.
	2. Kt. to K. B.'s 2nd
3. B. takes Kt.	3. Kt. takes Kt.
4. Kt. to K. B.'s 6th (mate)	

No. 161.

WHITE.	BLACK.
1. B. to K. B.'s 6th	1. B. to K. B.'s 7th, or (a)
2. B. takes K.'s P.	2. B. or Kt. checks
3. K. to Q. B.'s 4th (dis. ch.)	3. B. or Kt. covers
4. B. takes B. or Kt., and mates	

(a).

WHITE.	BLACK.
	1. P. " Queens "
2. B. to Q. B.'s 2nd (dis. ch.)	2. Q. to Q. Kt.'s 6th
3. R. takes Q. (ch.)	3. K. moves
4. Kt. mates	

Black's defences are many, besides those given above, but in every case mate is accomplished in four moves.

No. 162.

WHITE.	BLACK.
1. Kt. to K. B.'s 7th	1. K. to B.'s 3rd, or (a), (b)
2. Kt. to Q.'s 6th	2. K. to Q.'s 4th
3. B. to K.'s 3rd	3. Any move
4. R. mates	

(a).

WHITE.	BLACK.
	1. K. to R.'s 3rd
2. Kt. to Q.'s 6th	2. K. to R.'s 4th
3. R. to Q. B.'s 3rd	3. Anything
4. R. mates	

WHITE.	(b).	BLACK.
		1. Kt. moves
2. Kt. to Q.'s 6th (ch.)		2. K. to K. Kt.'s sq. or R.'s sq.
3. B. to K. Kt.'s sq.		3. Any move
4. R. mates		

No. 163.

WHITE.		BLACK.
1. R. to K.'s 2nd		1. K. takes K.'s P., or (a)
2. B. to K. R.'s 5th		2. K. to Q.'s 6th

(If Black play otherwise, then follows:—3. Kt. to K. Kt.'s 4th, and mate next move.)

WHITE.		BLACK.
3. Kt. to K. Kt.'s 2nd		3. Any move
4. Kt. mates		

(a).

WHITE.		BLACK.
		1. Kt. to Q.'s 3rd
2. K. takes Kt.		2. Any move
3. Kt. to K. Kt.'s 2nd, or Q. B.'s 2nd		3. Any move
4. Kt. mates		

No. 164.

WHITE.		BLACK.
1. B. to Q. Kt's 6th (ch.)		1. R. interposes (best)
2. Q. to K.'s 6th		2. P. takes Kt. (best)
3. Q. takes R. (ch.)		3. K. moves or Q. interposes
4. Q. to Q. R.'s 4th (mate)		

No. 165.

WHITE.		BLACK.
1. Kt. takes Q.'s P. (dis. ch.)		1. K. takes Kt. (best)
2. Kt. to Q. B.'s 6th		2. R. to K.'s 5th (best)
3. R. to Q.'s 4th (ch.)		3. R. takes R.
4. Kt. takes Kt. (mate)		

No. 166.

WHITE.		BLACK.
1. B. to Q.'s 4th		1. K. moves, or (a), (b)
2. K. to Q.'s 5th		2. K. to Q. B.'s 2nd
3. K. to K.'s 6th		3. Any move.
4. R. to Q. B.'s 8th (mate)		

(a).

WHITE.		BLACK.
		1. Kt. to K. R.'s 6th
2. K. to Q.'s 5th		2. Kt. checks
3. K. to Q. B.'s 6th		3. Any move
4. R. to K.'s 8th (mate)		

(b).

WHITE.		BLACK.
		1. P. moves
2. R. to K. R.'s 7th (ch.)		2. K. to B.'s sq.
3. K. to K.'s 6th		3. Any move
4. R. mates		

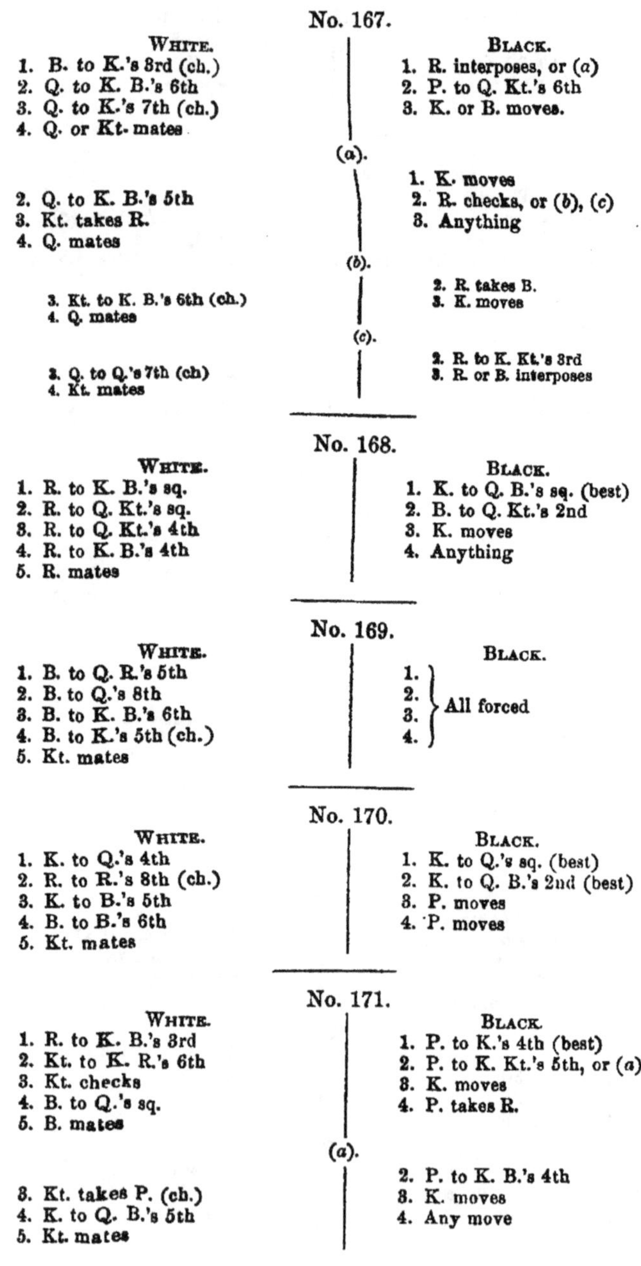

No. 167.

WHITE.	BLACK.
1. B. to K.'s 3rd (ch.)	1. R. interposes, or (a)
2. Q. to K. B.'s 6th	2. P. to Q. Kt.'s 6th
3. Q. to K.'s 7th (ch.)	3. K. or B. moves.
4. Q. or Kt. mates	

(a).

	1. K. moves
2. Q. to K. B.'s 5th	2. R. checks, or (b), (c)
3. Kt. takes R.	3. Anything
4. Q. mates	

(b).

	2. R. takes B.
3. Kt. to K. B.'s 6th (ch.)	3. K. moves
4. Q. mates	

(c).

	2. R. to K. Kt.'s 3rd
3. Q. to Q.'s 7th (ch)	3. R. or B. interposes
4. Kt. mates	

No. 168.

WHITE.	BLACK.
1. R. to K. B.'s sq.	1. K. to Q. B.'s sq. (best)
2. R. to Q. Kt.'s sq.	2. B. to Q. Kt.'s 2nd
3. R. to Q. Kt.'s 4th	3. K. moves
4. R. to K. B.'s 4th	4. Anything
5. R. mates	

No. 169.

WHITE.	BLACK.
1. B. to Q. R.'s 5th	1.
2. B. to Q.'s 8th	2.
3. B. to K. B.'s 6th	3. } All forced
4. B. to K.'s 5th (ch.)	4.
5. Kt. mates	

No. 170.

WHITE.	BLACK.
1. K. to Q.'s 4th	1. K. to Q.'s sq. (best)
2. R. to R.'s 8th (ch.)	2. K. to Q. B.'s 2nd (best)
3. K. to B.'s 5th	3. P. moves
4. B. to B.'s 6th	4. P. moves
5. Kt. mates	

No. 171.

WHITE.	BLACK.
1. R. to K. B.'s 3rd	1. P. to K.'s 4th (best)
2. Kt. to K. R.'s 6th	2. P. to K. Kt.'s 5th, or (a)
3. Kt. checks	3. K. moves
4. B. to Q.'s sq.	4. P. takes R.
5. B. mates	

(a).

	2. P. to K. B.'s 4th
3. Kt. takes P. (ch.)	3. K. moves
4. K. to Q. B.'s 5th	4. Any move
5. Kt. mates	

No. 172.

WHITE.	BLACK.
1. B. to Q. B.'s 7th (ch.)	1. K. to Q. B.'s sq.
2. B. to K. B.'s 4th (dis. ch.)	2. Q. takes R., or (a)
3. B. to K. Kt.'s 4th	3. Q. takes Q. (ch.)*
4. K. to K.'s 7th (dis. ch.)	4. Q. interposes
5. B. takes Q. (mate)	

(a).

	2. R. takes R.
3. Q. takes P. (ch.)	3. K. moves
4. Q. to K.'s 7th (ch.)	4. K. moves
5. Q. mates	

* If Black play Q. to Q. B.'s 2nd, White replies with K. to K. B.'s 6th (dis. ch.), and mates next move.

No. 173.

WHITE.	BLACK.
1. B. to Q. B.'s sq.	1.
2. B. to K. R.'s 6th	2.
3. B. to K. B.'s 8th	3. } All forced.
4. B. to Q. Kt.'s 5th (ch.)	4.
5. Kt. mates	

No. 174.

WHITE.	BLACK.
1. B. to Q. R.'s sq.	1. K. to Q. B.'s 5th*
2. Kt. to Q.'s 4th (dis. ch.)	2. K. to Q.'s 6th, or (a)
3. B. to Q. B.'s 3rd	3. Any move
4. B. to K.'s sq.	4. Any move
5. R. mates	

(a).

	2. K. to Q. Kt.'s 5th
3. B. to Q. B.'s 3rd (ch.)	3. K. to Q. B.'s 4th or Q. R.'s
4. B. to Q. R.'s 5th (dis. ch.), or	5th

R. to Q. R.'s sq. (mate) according to Black's play

* Black may vary his defence, but play as he can, the result will be the same.

T. F. A. DAY, PRINTER, 13, CAREY STREET, LINCOLN'S INN.